This book belongs to

_____

Date I started this study

_____

> This is the companion study for the group study with the same title. It is ideal for individual learners as they follow along in the group study. The group study is delivered online. Go to lifebiblestudy.com for more information.

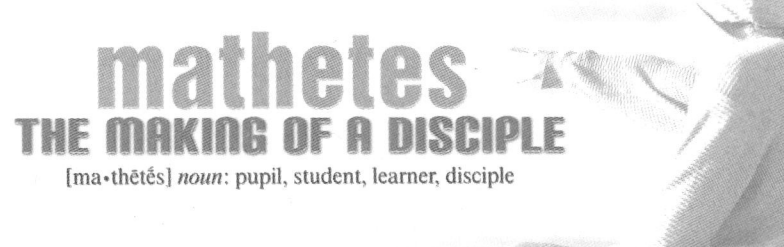

mathetes
THE MAKING OF A DISCIPLE
[ma·thētés] *noun*: pupil, student, learner, disciple

mathetes
THE MAKING OF A DISCIPLE
[ma·thētēs] *noun*: pupil, student, learner, disciple

NavPress is the publishing ministry of The Navigators, an international Christian organization and leader in personal spiritual development. NavPress is committed to helping people grow spiritually and enjoy lives of meaning and hope through personal and group resources that are biblically rooted, culturally relevant, and highly practical.

For a free catalog go to www.NavPress.com or call 1.800.366.7788 in the United States or 1.800.839.4769 in Canada.

© 2013 by The Navigators

All rights reserved. No part of this publication may be reproduced in any form without the written permission from NavPress, P.O. Box 35001, Colorado Springs, CO 80935. www.navpress.com

NavPress, the NAVPRESS logo, Life Bible Study, and the Life Bible Study logo are registered trademarks of NavPress. Absence of ® in connection with marks of NavPress or other parties does not indicate an absence of registration of those marks.

ISBN-13: 978-1-61291-570-8

Cover design: Jennifer Myers

Editor: Margie Williamson

Some of the anecdotal illustrations in this book are true to life and are included with the permission of the persons involved. All other illustrations are composites of real situations, and any resemblance to people living or dead is coincidental.

Unless otherwise noted, all Scriptures quotations are taken from the Holy Bible, New International Version. Copyright © 1973, 1978, 1984, 2011 by International Bible Society. Used by Permission. All rights reserved.

TABLE OF CONTENTS

Introduction

Unit 1   LIVING IN WORSHIP
week 1: The One We Worship
week 2: The Author of Worship
week 3: An Audience of One
week 4: The Ever-Present Spirit
week 5: Sacrificial Worship
week 6: Worship is Forever

Unit 2   UNDERTAKING HOLY DISCIPLINES
week 7: The Discipline of Prayer
week 8: The Discipline of Scripture Study
week 9: The Discipline of Fasting
week 10: The Discipline of Giving
week 11: The Discipline of Meditation
week 12: The Discipline of Sabbath

Unit 3   USING GOD'S GIFTS WISELY
week 13: Gifted with Time
week 14: Gifted with Skills
week 15: Gifted with Contentment
week 16: Gifted for Him
week 17: Gifted for the Body
week 18: Gifted to Love

Unit 4   ACTING OUT FAITH
week 19: Growing Faith
week 20: Integrated Faith
week 21: Pure and Undefiled Faith
week 22: Obedient Faith
week 23: Verbal Faith
week 24: Imitated Faith

Unit 5   COMING BACK TO GOD
week 25: Confess Sin
week 26: Accept Consequences
week 27: Repent and Move Forward
week 28: Find Restoration
week 29: Reconcile with Others
week 30: Represent God Anew

Unit 6 RELATING TO OTHERS
week 31: Made for Each Other
week 32: Love One Another
week 33: In Relationship
week 34: Relationships that Last
week 35: Unified Together
week 36: Mutual Respect

Unit 7 DISCIPLING OTHERS
week 37: Teach By Example
week 38: Testify to the Gospel
week 39: Teaching What is Right
week 40: Serve the World/Love Others
week 41: Do Good to Others
week 42: Show Mercy

Unit 8 THE BRIDGE TO MISSIONS
week 43: Reason Together
week 44: Righteous Wrath
week 45: Quick Grace
week 46: Safe and Secure
week 47: Suffering Servant
week 48: Free Future

Conclusion

INTRODUCTION
MATHETES: THE MAKING OF A DISCIPLE
[ma•thetes] noun: pupil, student, learner, disciple

Randy had not grown up in a church and knew nothing about faith. When he started as a freshman at the University of Georgia, his dorm was located directly across the street from the Baptist Student Center. The center had a television, ping pong table, coffee, and donuts. Randy and his buddies began spending all their free time at the center and became regulars around the coffee pot. One day, over donuts, Randy began asking questions; he wondered what Christianity was really about. Another student, an upper classman, answered his questions and, after several months of discussion, Randy made a decision to follow Christ.

Randy's journey didn't end there. He was given a Bible and he began spending his free time devouring the Word of God instead of playing ping pong or watching television. I remember walking into the center between classes and seeing Randy curled up on a sofa, Bible in hand. The upper classman who had led Randy to Christ continued to spend time with him, answering his questions, explaining passages that were hard to understand, and helping him know what was required of him as a believer. Randy's decision to follow Christ became the first step on his journey to become a disciple of Christ; the upper classman who worked with Randy demonstrated the role of one disciple mentoring another. I watched the process of discipleship in that relationship for years.

In Psalm 119, David created a literary masterpiece about the importance of God's Word. In verse 9, the psalmist asked how anyone could stay pure. His answer was based on God's Word and also provides a picture of the process of discipleship: "By living according to your word. I seek you with all my heart; do not let me stray from your commands. I have hidden your word in my heart that I might not sin against you." (verses 9b-11).

David pointed out three actions that are involved with following God: (1) study His Word; (2) live out God's instructions; and (3) continue to seek God's heart in all we do. Even Jesus used His knowledge of Scripture to face His time of temptation in the wilderness: Jesus answered, "It is written: 'Man shall not live on bread alone, but on every word that comes from the mouth of God.'" (Matthew 4:4). And Jesus spent His time on earth teaching and discipling His disciples so they would be prepared to lead others in discipleship.

Discipleship is a journey and life-long

7

process. It involves daily seeking to know God's heart, studying God's Word, and then living out God's expectations. It is not an easy journey, but it is more rewarding than any other endeavor in this life.

This book is a collection of devotions that will help you evaluate where you are on this journey. The book is divided into eight units that highlight areas of a disciple's growth: Living in Worship; Undertaking Holy Disciplines; Using God's Gifts Wisely; Acting Out Faith; Coming Back to God; Relating to Others; Discipling Others; and The Bridge to Missions. Each unit includes six chapters pinpointing specific portions within each area of growth; each chapter contains five daily devotions to guide you at every step of your journey.

You may choose to complete your weekly devotions in preparation for your upcoming Bible study, or afterwards as a way to meditate on the passage just studied as a group.

The following suggestions will help you get the most out of your study:

- Use your favorite Bible as your primary study Bible, but have several other translations handy to allow you to read assigned passages from different translations.
- Experiment with different study locations. Spend time outside while you study as well as places in which you haven't previously studied inside your house or office. Often, a change in scenery will make you more sensitive to God's presence.
- Don't hesitate to respond honestly to the questions provided in each devotion. Your answers are between you and God alone. You will not be asked to share them with anyone.
- Consider adding a small notebook to your study materials so you can journal at least weekly about what you are learning about God and about yourself through your study.

Mathetes: The Making of a Disciple is a guide for every believer in the journey of maturity and multiplication ...from personal worship and spiritual disciplines to lifestyles of faith and intentional relationships. Be prepared to consider, examine, and evaluate God's Word as you move through this study.

As I worked on this book, I couldn't help but think of observing discipleship in progress in the lives of Randy and his mentor. Our prayer is that this study will give you the opportunity to better understand what God wants of us as disciples, to seek to know God's heart, and to share that knowledge by discipling others.

Margie Williamson, Editor

STATEMENTS OF FAITH

When studying the Bible, broad themes, or essential truths, become obvious. These themes become the foundation for understanding who God is and how He has revealed Himself. Life Bible Study curriculum is designed to highlight eight truths that are essential in understanding the character and work of God.

God Is

Only one true and living God exists. He is the Creator of the universe, eternally existing in three Persons —the Father, Son, and Holy Spirit— each equally deserving of humanity's worship and obedience. He is infinite and perfect in all His attributes.

The Bible is God's Word

The Bible is God's written revelation to people, divinely given through human authors who were inspired by the Holy Spirit. It is entirely true. The Bible is totally sufficient and completely authoritative for matters of life and faith. The goal of God's Word is the restoration of humanity into His image.

People are God's Treasure

God created people in His image for His glory. They are the crowning work of His creation. Yet every person has willfully disobeyed God—an act known as sin—thus inheriting both physical and spiritual death and the need for salvation. All human beings are born with a sin-nature and into an environment inclined toward sin. Only by the grace of God through Jesus Christ can they experience salvation.

Jesus is God and Savior

Jesus is both fully God and fully human. He is Christ, the Son of God. Born of a virgin, He lived a sinless life and performed many miracles. He died on the cross to provide people forgiveness of sin and eternal salvation. Jesus rose from the dead, ascended to the right hand of the Father, and will return in power and glory.

The Holy Spirit is God and Empowerer

The Holy Spirit is supernatural and sovereign, baptizing all believers into the Body of Christ. He lives within all Christians beginning at the moment of salvation and then empowers them for bold witness and effective service as they yield to Him. The Holy Spirit convicts individuals of sin, uses God's Word to mature believers into Christ-likeness, and secures them until Christ returns.

Salvation is by Faith Alone

All human beings are born with a sin nature, separated from God, and in need of a Savior. That salvation comes only through a faith relationship with Jesus Christ, the Savior, as a person repents of sin and receives Christ's forgiveness and eternal life. Salvation is instantaneous and accomplished solely by the power of the Holy Spirit through the Word of God. This salvation is wholly of God by grace on the basis of the shed blood of Jesus Christ and not on the basis of human works. All the redeemed are secure in Christ forever.

The Church is God's Plan

The Holy Spirit immediately places all people who put their faith in Jesus Christ into one united spiritual body, the Church, of which Christ is the head. The primary expression of the Church on earth is in autonomous local congregations of baptized believers. The purpose of the Church is to glorify God by taking the gospel to the entire world and by building its members up in Christ-likeness through the instruction of God's Word, fellowship, service, worship, and prayer.

The Future is in God's Hands

God will bring the world to its appropriate end in His own time and in His own way. At that time, Jesus Christ will return personally and visibly in glory to the earth. Both the saved and unsaved will be resurrected physically to be judged by Christ. Those who have trusted Christ will receive their reward and dwell forever in heaven with the Lord. Those who have refused Christ will spend eternity in hell, the place of everlasting punishment. The certain return of Christ motivates believers to be faithful in their daily lives.

LIVING IN WORSHIP
Week 1: *The One We Worship*
DRESSED IN GLORY   Psalm 104:1-4

Praise the LORD, my soul. LORD my God, you are very great; you are clothed with splendor and majesty. The LORD wraps himself in light as with a garment; he stretches out the heavens like a tent and lays the beams of his upper chambers on their waters. He makes the clouds his chariot and rides on the wings of the wind. He makes winds his messengers, flames of fire his servants.

Every great song has a beginning that captures your attention, a middle that carries the tune, and a hook which bridges the song through and back to an uplifting chorus. In this passage we experience a song that describes the full glory of God. The writer uses a metaphor, a picture of how he sees God, dressing for the day.

Worship of God begins with an acknowledgement that God is, indeed, great! The visual picture here is stunning. You can almost see God stretching out His arms through His sleeves of light and pushing out cobalt blue skies as His home. The depths of the oceans, fearful even to modern man, are nothing to this master builder. His location is not dependent upon ancient effort. He is as free as the wind.

Spend a moment imagining the splendor and majesty of God. What impresses you about Him? What fears does a God like this ignite within you? What peace do you find, knowing a God like Him? Jot down your thoughts below.

PRAYER
Heavenly Father, your glory is revealed in the heavens. Your majesty is majestic and matchless. You are a great and mighty God. You O Lord are indeed great and worthy of all praise. Amen.

_____

_____

_____

_____

LIVING IN WORSHIP
Week 1: *The One We Worship*
FROLICKING IN THE OCEAN   Psalm 104:24-28

How many are your works, LORD! In wisdom you made them all; the earth is full of your creatures. There is the sea, vast and spacious, teeming with creatures beyond number—living things both large and small. There the ships go to and fro, and Leviathan, which you formed to frolic there. All creatures look to you to give them their food at the proper time. When you give it to them, they gather it up; when you open your hand, they are satisfied with good things.

On a trip to Alaska, we got to experience the wonder of watching and listening to a pod of whales as they hunted together. We watched amazed as they broke the water time after time, and then were stunned as one breached just off to the right of our boat. It was a spiritual moment as we watched the power and the beauty of God's creation.

Compared to what we know about the sea today, the psalmist knew little about the ocean and the fish and animals that lived there. But stories of those, including the power of the Leviathan, a huge animal that must have been like a whale, that frolicked in that huge playground gave evidence of the power of the Creator God. When reflecting upon the beauty of the oceans, the teeming life that thrived there, and the power of that life, the psalmist could only give praise to the God of all creation...including the Leviathan.

Reflect on a time when you stood beside the crashing waves of the ocean, or when you stood on a deck on a boat out on the ocean. Did you feel small before the evidence of God's creation? How would you share the spiritual impact of that moment with one who has yet to recognize God as Creator of all things? How can you respond to God now for His creation of the oceans, the seas, and all those that dwell within? Write that response below.

PRAYER
Heavenly Father, You alone have the power to create the oceans, to fill it with life and beauty, to make it a place in which Your glory is revealed. You are my God, the Creator of all that I see and touch and hear. You are above all things on earth and in the seas. May I never lose my sense of awe when confronted with Your creation. Amen.

_____

_____

_____

LIVING IN WORSHIP
Week 1: *The One We Worship*

GOD'S OPEN HAND
Psalm 104:27-30

All creatures look to you to give them their food at the proper time. When you give it to them, they gather it up; when you open your hand, they are satisfied with good things. When you hide your face, they are terrified; when you take away their breath, they die and return to the dust. When you send your Spirit, they are created, and you renew the face of the ground.

We live on an old homestead that my grandfather built, surrounded by almost 100 acres of timber and forest. We can't miss seeing God's provision in this place, from the apple and pear trees my grandparents planted, and the wild scuppernong, muscadine, and persimmon vines scattered in the woods that feed both us and the deer and wildlife, to even the acorns which feed the squirrels. God's care for His creation in evident in our little part of His world.

All creation, not just mankind, is dependent upon God's provision to survive and thrive. We are dependent on God's actions—He gives and satisfies, sends His Spirit, renews the earth—just as creation was dependent upon God for its' very beginning. God's creation is not a once-upon-a-time act, but a continuing process of provision and renewal. And all of it points to one thing...to God, the Creator and Sustainer of us all.

Pause and look out a window. What evidence of God's creation do you see before you? How will that evidence change with the seasons? Below, describe God's world as you see it, right this minute. And then praise Him for that world, for the changes you get to see as you move through each season, and for the way He continues to provide for you physically and sustain you spiritually through His creation.

PRAYER
Father, God, Creator, Lord, You created a dwelling place for me that is more beautiful than I could have ever imagined, that teems with life that demonstrates Your love in the very details You included, and that provides everything that we and all Your creatures need to thrive. May I never forget to stop and revel in the glory of Your world. Amen.

_____

_____

_____

13

LIVING IN WORSHIP
Week 1: *The One We Worship*
HIS GLORY ENDURES FOREVER   Psalm 104:31–32

May the glory of the LORD endure forever; may the LORD rejoice in his works—he who looks at the earth, and it trembles, who touches the mountains, and they smoke.

I'm a Georgia boy who grew up loving the mountains. But it wasn't until my first trip to the Rockies that I realized that the mountains of Georgia are more like foothills when compared to the rugged mountains in the west. The explorers Lewis and Clark recorded their shock when they traveled for so long toward the Rockies...they could not comprehend the size of the mountain range from first sight. I now understand that feeling.

Yet, the psalmist recorded that even God's creation...the earth covered in great land masses and huge oceans, the tall mountains before which man is dwarfed...trembles in awesome fear before the Lord. The Rocky Mountains are over 3,000 miles long, stretching from British Columbia to New Mexico, and are more than 55 million years old. God's glory does indeed endure forever. How greatly He deserves our praise!

Think of the first time you saw some incredible geographical or geological attraction—a mountain, a waterfall, a rock formation, a canyon. Do you remember how you felt as you stood before it or looked over it? Describe those feelings as you remember them. Did you stop and think of the One who created or were you just focused on the creation itself? How does the way you view creation indicate the way you view the Creator? Would you approach that evidence of God the same way at this stage of your life? Why?

PRAYER
God, You created the mountains, the sky that surrounds them, the birds that fly above them, and all that dwell upon it. And all that You created reflects Your glory, Your power, and Your love for us. Lord, please show me how to love You more by seeing Your glory in all that is around me. Amen.

LIVING IN WORSHIP
Week 1: *The One We Worship*
HIS GLORY ENDURES FOREVER   Psalm 104:33-35

I will sing to the LORD all my life; I will sing praise to my God as long as I live. May my meditation be pleasing to him, as I rejoice in the LORD. But may sinners vanish from the earth and the wicked be no more. Praise the LORD, my soul. Praise the LORD.

At a recent family camping trip, four generations came together in worship. We sat in camp chairs around a campfire and sang songs of praise that we've shared together for years. There were even a few favorite hymns sung to remember family members who have already passed on. There were no musical instruments, except for the morning birdsong from the trees and the gurgle of the nearby stream. There was no preacher, except for the testimonies and praises of those sitting around the fire. It wasn't a skilled time of worship, but it was one of the sweetest I've ever experienced. And I believe that time of praise was sweet for God as well.

The psalmist had only one response to God and His creation...his personal praise and worship of the Almighty God, the Creator and Sustainer of the universe. He described his worship using active words—sing, meditate, rejoice, praise. He proclaimed that he would sing to the Lord for the rest of his life, meditate upon the Lord, and rejoice in Him. And he asked that his meditation, the time he spent thinking about God, be pleasing to Him.

If the weather allows, take your Bible and this book outside into God's creation. If not, pull your chair up to the window and look into God's creation. Think about God. What do you want to say to Him right now? Read all of Psalm 104 aloud as a prayer, rereading those statements that seem to reflect what you are feeling right now. When you've finished, write your answer to the question above.

PRAYER
God, I recognize Your glory that is revealed through Your creation. I rejoice that I am allowed to immerse myself in Your world. I praise you as the Lord and Creator of all. Amen.

LIVING IN WORSHIP
Week 2: *The Author of Worship*
YOU MUST...REALLY   Deuteronomy 5:6–7

I am the LORD your God, who brought you out of Egypt, out of the land of slavery. You shall have no other gods before me.

As a kid, my sister Jan was helping my mom in the kitchen. Mom asked her if the stove was on. Instead of looking at the control on the stove, Jan put her hand directly on the burner. Her hand was seared, and the family had a new rule: Do not put your hand on a burner to find out if the stove is on. You'd think that's so obvious it wouldn't need to become a rule. Jan's action proved otherwise. Because my parents had seen the worst results possible from her mistake, they didn't want any one else to suffer. The rule was meant to prevent further mistakes, further consequences, further pain ...further suffering.

Check the word *shall* in the dictionary and you'll find it explained in terms of "mandatory actions" and what "must" be done. No adult wants to be told what he or she must or must not do. In today's culture, many look for the gray room in any rule that can allow a level of personal interpretation, such as you're only really speeding if you more than eight miles over the speed limit. But God gave a list of must and must not commandments which are not open to interpretation. And the regulations were given because God wanted to prevent the mistakes that can lead to pain and suffering. The first commandment is the most important and the other nine help us understand what that first commandment entails. It's a non-negotiable, non-interpretable requirement that must (not should) be obeyed.

Look at the first commandment carefully. What does this mean to you today? Rewrite it below by replacing the words "no other gods" with the things in your life that get in the way of your relationship with God. Have you attempted to interpret this commandment so it fits your life, rather than how your life fits God's requirements? Why? If you were to be completely obedient to His requirement, what changes *must* you make?

PRAYER
God, You deserve my unwavering, steadfast devotion, for You alone are God. Help me see where I have missed the mark, where I have rationalized my actions, where I have justified my lack of obedience. Please, Lord, remind me daily that I am Yours alone. Amen.

LIVING IN WORSHIP
Week 2: *The Author of Worship*
DON'T DO IT
Deuteronomy 5:8–15

You shall not make for yourself an image in the form of anything in heaven above or on the earth beneath or in the waters below. You shall not bow down to them or worship them; for I, the Lord your God, am a jealous God, punishing the children for the sin of the parents to the third and fourth generation of those who hate me, but showing love to a thousand generations of those who love me and keep my commandments. You shall not misuse the name of the Lord your God, for the Lord will not hold anyone guiltless who misuses his name. Observe the Sabbath day by keeping it holy, as the Lord your God has commanded you. Six days you shall labor and do all your work, but the seventh day is a sabbath to the Lord your God. On it you shall not do any work, neither you, nor your son or daughter, nor your male or female servant, nor your ox, your donkey or any of your animals, nor any foreigner residing in your towns, so that your male and female servants may rest, as you do. Remember that you were slaves in Egypt and that the Lord your God brought you out of there with a mighty hand and an outstretched arm. Therefore the Lord your God has commanded you to observe the Sabbath day.

Relationships are tricky to maintain. There are things that have to be done to maintain a relationship—spending time on it, developing trust, making it a priority. Think how many relationships in your life are no longer strong because these have been neglected. There are other things that cannot be done without injuring the relationship —like hurting the other person, breaking trust, being unavailable. Every relationship thrives to the extent that these "do" and "do not" areas are honored.

God's first commandment set the basis for our relationship with Him...there can be nothing in our lives more important than He is. And the next three flesh out what that means: Don't try to be god yourself by creating your own things you honor; don't dishonor God by using His name in vain; and take time out every week to put priority time in building an ever-growing, ever-improving relationship with God.

Take a look at each of these three requirements. Are there areas in your life that have fallen victim to any of these? Do you try to create for yourself, rather than depending upon God? Do you dishonor Him in your speech or actions? Is your Sabbath-time in Him and with Him your top priority each week? Answer each of these questions below, indicating both where you presently are and where you would like to be in your relationship with God.

PRAYER
God, show me Your ways. Teach me Your commands. Convict me of my short-comings, my areas of arrogance, my times of neglect, my times when I take our relationship for granted. Help me become the person You would have me to be. Amen.

LIVING IN WORSHIP
Week 2: *The Author of Worship*

SHOW RESPECT Deuteronomy 5:16–22

Honor your father and your mother, as the LORD your God has commanded you, so that you may live long and that it may go well with you in the land the LORD your God is giving you. You shall not murder. You shall not commit adultery. You shall not steal. You shall not give false testimony against your neighbor. You shall not covet your neighbor's wife. You shall not set your desire on your neighbor's house or land, his male or female servant, his ox or donkey, or anything that belongs to your neighbor. These are the commandments the LORD proclaimed in a loud voice to your whole assembly there on the mountain from out of the fire, the cloud and the deep darkness; and he added nothing more. Then he wrote them on two stone tablets and gave them to me.

Years ago, our home was broken into as thieves busted out a window behind the house. They stole everything they could carry...as well as something they couldn't —our sense of security. Months later, the house was broken into a second time. The stuff that was taken could easily be replaced. The lost sense of security was much harder to get beyond. It took years before we could emotionally move beyond that. And the years of struggle for us were the result of people who had no care about us but only what they wanted at the time.

How we treat others is important to God. In fact, it's so important that God provided more requirements for how we are to relate to others than for how we are to relate to Him. First, He commands that we honor–respect–our parents. And then He commands that we treat others with respect—don't murder someone, don't steal the things they own, don't injure or even destroy a marital relationship with adultery, and don't injure someone's reputation. Each of these are personal injuries...they damage families, they challenge a family's sense of safety, they can even destroy a family's ability to take care of itself.

It's easy to look at these requirements and check the first few off. Most of us care about our parents and we'd never consider taking a life or breaking and entering into someone's house or business. But if we look at these closely, we probably do have things we've done that have not respected what belongs to others. Have we taken over someone's responsibilities because we didn't think he or she did it well enough? Have we talked about someone in a way that injured his or her reputation? Have you been unwilling to listen to someone else's point of view? You get the picture...Prayerfully consider how you demonstrate respect to others, and possibly how you don't. Below, record your conclusions.

PRAYER
God, do I respect others in all ways? Do I represent Your love in the way I treat others? Have I let You down in my actions, my words, my neglect, my arrogance, or even my self-righteousness. Lord, show me where I've let You down and convict me when I fail You. Amen.

LIVING IN WORSHIP
Week 2: *The Author of Worship*

WITH OUR WHOLE SELVES Deuteronomy 6:4–5

Hear, O Israel: The LORD our God, the LORD is one. Love the LORD your God with all your heart and with all your soul and with all your strength.

My wife and my grandson have a ritual they go through when they say, "I love you," to the other. One says, "I love you," and the other replies, "Well, I love you more." It's a simple exercise that really communicates one idea to the other—that each is loved sincerely, completely, and knows that love is reciprocated. Imagine if that exercise was done with God. We can say, "I love you" to God, and His response will always be, "I love you more...more than you can even comprehend." Such is the amazing, overwhelming, inconceivable love of God for us.

And what does God expect of us? He expects our love in return, a love that embraces our very being, the complete totality of who we are. He described this love as coming from the heart, the soul, and from our strength. These words are not meant to symbolize emotions or physical powers. Rather, they represent the Old Testament understanding of the essence of who we are. We are to love God completely with our whole beings. It is the love that God demonstrated to us through His Son. And it is the love that Jesus recalled when He talked to the young man who thought he already met all of God's requirements (see Matthew 22:37-38).

What does loving God with your whole being mean to you? Below, describe what that looks like in your life. Then, read what you wrote with your understanding of how God loves you. Describe the love of God for you. Then, compare the two and prayerfully consider what God would have you do with your comparisons.

PRAYER
God, I know You love me beyond my expectations, beyond my comprehension, and way beyond what I deserve. Help me to know what it means to love You in the way You deserve. And help me be able to demonstrate that love in a way that is worthy of You. Amen.

LIVING IN WORSHIP
Week 2: *The Author of Worship*

PASSING ON THE FAITH — Deuteronomy 6:6–9

These commandments that I give you today are to be on your hearts. Impress them on your children. Talk about them when you sit at home and when you walk along the road, when you lie down and when you get up. Tie them as symbols on your hands and bind them on your foreheads. Write them on the doorframes of your houses and on your gates.

When my wife and I found out that we were expecting our first child, we were somewhat overwhelmed at the responsibility that was coming our way. We talked about what we hoped for our child and actually discussed how we would know that we had succeeded when that child was grown. As we talked, we never thought about things like grades or careers...only about what it would mean for him to be a godly man with a relationship with God that would be demonstrated in how he treated others.

Deuteronomy 6:4–9 is often referred to as *the Shema*, and describes how God holds the family accountable for passing their faith in God to the next generations. Many Jews continue to bind or tie leather boxes containing sacred Scripture to the arm and the forehead as a reminder of the importance of God's word. And they accept responsibility for teaching their children about God. If there is one glaring weakness in the Christian faith, it is the lack of parental involvement in teaching children about God. Too often, that responsibility is passed on to workers within the church, whether these are ministers or laypeople.

A text used to train ministers to work with children states that Christianity is never more than one generation away from extinction. Why? Because every child must be taught who God is and what God did for them through His Son. Without that teaching, they may never hear. What role do you play in passing on your faith to the next generations in your family or even your church family? Reread the statement at the beginning of this paragraph, pray about the significance of that responsibility, and then record below what God puts on your heart in response.

PRAYER

Heavenly Father, You've shown us what it means to love children, to sacrificially love them completely, and to shoulder the responsibility of introducing them to You. Lord, help us see opportunities to take on that responsibility. Amen.

LIVING IN WORSHIP
Week 3: *An Audience of One*
SHOUT OUT
Psalm 100:1–2

Shout for joy to the LORD, all the earth. Worship the LORD with gladness; come before him with joyful songs.

On a pilgrimage to Israel, I witnessed a wedding ceremony outside my hotel room in Jerusalem. I have never witnessed such a combination of joy and worship. I didn't understand a word that was said during the ceremony, but I stood entranced as I watched all those involved—rabbis, friends, family members, bride and groom—participate joyfully. There was dancing and singing and shouting and prayers...and at the end of the ceremony the bride and groom were carried off on perches, surrounded by a singing, dancing, celebrating mob of friends. I watched until the last person disappeared and couldn't help but notice how empty the scene felt when all had left.

In Psalm 100, I believe the psalmist was picturing such a scene of worship as he wrote. Scholars believe the psalm was used as a hymn and was sung during religious festivals—like that wedding I saw, or the Feasts of Tabernacles, or any of the other festivals that celebrated God's enduring presence in the lives of His people in Israel. All of the acts within that celebration pointed to one thing—worship and praise for the True God by every creature on the earth.

Read Luke 19:37-44 and picture what Jesus' triumphal entry into Jerusalem must have looked like. And then, reread verse 40: "I tell you," he replied, "if they [the disciples and the people celebrating Jesus' arrival] keep quiet, the stones will cry out." The psalmist proclaimed that ALL the earth was to shout out their praise of God. Below, record your statement of praise and worship that responds to this imperative. And then, try shouting out that praise before God. Experience what it can mean to let go of your inhibitions in order to express your deepest feelings about God.

PRAYER
You alone are my God and I shout that knowledge out for all to hear. You alone have the ability to create all I see and provide all I have and I worship You as the Creator and Sustainer of all that is. May I never forget to worship You in joy and gladness. Amen.

_____
_____
_____
_____

LIVING IN WORSHIP
Week 3: *An Audience of One*

I WANT TO BE A SHEEP   Psalm 100:3

Know that the Lord is God. It is he who made us, and we are his; we are his people, the sheep of his pasture.

I came into close contact with sheep for the first time at a wide place in the road in Israel. They looked cute and docile until they got close up. Then, I couldn't get over how "sheep-y" they smelled. Think of a long-haired, wet, dirty dog. Sheep also seemed pretty helpless. I watched as their herders kept them from running in front of cars on the highway. I also watched as the sheep obediently followed their handlers to safety. For me, it was a moment that clarified the picture of God's sheep in the Psalms.

The psalmist emphasized that God's people, His sheep, are to "know" God, meaning we are to recognize that God is the one and only Lord of all, and that we are to confess (admit, declare) that recognition. And that confession makes us His sheep. We are not God's sheep because we are helpless or smelly. We are His sheep because He looks over us, He keeps us from harm, and He provides pastureland for us to dwell in, graze in, run in—yes, in which to live complete lives. We are His sheep: to follow Him where He leads, to trust Him in His provision and care, and to love and worship Him completely. And not to carry the analogy too far, but isn't it nice to know that He loves us in spite of the fact that we often smell bad before Him?

Read Psalm 23:1–4 and meditate on the picture of God's protection and care for us. Then, write below what that relationship between you and God is like by using the following words to spur your thoughts: loyal, obedient, follower, refreshed, and guided.

PRAYER
Lord, You are my Shepherd and I lack nothing. Help me recognize what that means. You give me green pastures and quiet waters. Help me appreciate those gifts in life. You refresh my soul. Help me be renewed daily through Your Word. You guide my way. Help me accept Your guidance in my life. Amen.

_____

_____

_____

_____

LIVING IN WORSHIP
Week 3: *An Audience of One*
HOW WE ENTER
Psalm 100:4

Enter his gates with thanksgiving and his courts with praise; give thanks to him and praise his name.

I love watching people enter our sanctuary on Sundays. They're happy to be there and greet each other in that way that only Christians who have known each other for many years and have walked beside each other in those years can do. But, they also reach out to those they don't know, welcoming them into that time of worship. It always feels like "old-home" week for me...and it happens every time we meet in worship.

The psalmist pictured the ritual of coming through the gates into God's Temple for worship as he wrote verse 4. Those who did not live in Jerusalem made a trip once or twice a year to worship in the Temple. They traveled in groups of family members and with those from their extended community. They sang together as they ascended into Jerusalem. Can you imagine the joy they must have felt when they arrived in the Holy City of Jerusalem and finally at the Temple? And they came to offer praises and sacrifices of thanksgiving.

What does entering your place of worship mean to you? Is it a celebration? A rite of tradition? What emotions do you experience? What attitude do you bring to that time of worship? Use these prompts below as you evaluate your worship experiences. Then, use your evaluations as you prepare for the coming worship services in the next few days.

PRAYER
Lord, I worship You as my God. I praise You because You deserve my unending praise. I come before You with the overwhelming thanks because I recognize and appreciate the blessings that come from You. Amen.

LIVING IN WORSHIP
Week 3: *An Audience of One*
FOREVER IS A LONG TIME Psalm 100:5a

For the LORD is good and his love endures forever.

Have you read the children's book, *I Love You Forever*? It's a beautiful picture of the love between parent and child that continues to grow throughout a lifetime. And for those of us who have lost a parent or a child, we know clearly that our love continues on after one has died. That love is eternal. Our love for those closest to us is but a shadow of the love that God has for us...and His love brings a new understanding of what can endure forever.

God loved us before we were born and even before the creation of the world. Scientists and creationists debate the age of the earth. Their estimates range from over six thousand years to four and a half BILLION years. With either argument, God has loved us in such a way that, throughout all the time in which people disappointed Him, He sent His Son to become our saving grace. And He continues to love us to such an extent that He allows us to spend the rest of eternity with Him. His love for us has been in evidence throughout all of history and will be throughout all of eternity. That certainly stretches my understanding of what is forever.

Meditate on the fact that God has loved you forever, not only globally through the creation of the world, but personally through the gift of His Son. Also, meditate on God's involvement in your life as described in Psalm 139:13: For you created my inmost being; you knit me together in my mother's womb. What does that tell you about God's love? Respond below.

PRAYER
Lord, You know me. You've always known me. You love me. You've always loved me and You always will love me. Teach me what that loves means. Amen.

_____

_____

_____

_____

_____

LIVING IN WORSHIP
Week 3: *An Audience of One*
THE GENERATIONS Psalm 100:5b

His faithfulness continues through all generations.

Generational theorists have worked hard to explain the way our current generations relate to each other. Terms like *baby boomers*, *gen xers*, and *millenialists* have become part of our current terminology. Theorists Strauss and Howe have even labeled generations back to the year 1433, a total of 25 generations. The question that is now being asked is how many generations have existed since the beginning of mankind. At this point, the question seems unanswerable but the possibilities could go into the millions.

The psalmist recognized that God's love passed from generation to generation (remember the study of *the Shema* last week) through understanding God's faithfulness. Probably no better picture of faith being passed from generation to generation can be found than the illustration given in Hebrews 11. Those who are recorded as the faithful are seen as such because of their response to and reflection of God's faithful participation in their lives. Hebrews 11 is a roll call of the faithful from the Old Testament. It is not a complete list.

Read Hebrews 11. Then, meditate on the faithful whose lives you've been able to witness. Add their names to the roll of the faithful by writing them below. Give thanks to God for the witness of their faithfulness and their testimonies of God's faithfulness.

PRAYER
My Father God who is in heaven, Holy is Your name. May Your kingdom come on earth and in heaven, just as You have planned. May I never take Your faithfulness for granted. Amen.

_____

_____

_____

_____

LIVING IN WORSHIP
Week 4: *The Ever-Present Spirit*

WORSHIP WARS

John 4:19-20

"Sir," the woman said, "I can see that you are a prophet. Our ancestors worshiped on this mountain, but you Jews claim that the place where we must worship is in Jerusalem."

It seems that one of the major challenges to churches today is how to worship. Generational preferences have become divisive elements in congregations. There's the type of worship issues—traditional, formal, contemporary, informal. There's the type of music—hymns, choral, choruses, praise bands. There's the place of worship itself—sanctuary, chapel, lunchroom, school building. Often, the decision to participate or even attend is based on whether the worship reflects those personal preferences. Want to start an argument? Get a young adult and a senior adult together and let them try to plan a worship service. Those different preferences are pretty ingrained in each individual's DNA.

When Jesus talked to the Samaritan woman at the well, the first thing she wanted to know was if He would accept her beliefs about where to worship. It was Worship Wars in its earliest form. The Samaritans had created their own place of worship at Mt. Gerizim, an action the Jews resented. But if you go back and read verses 7-18, you'll see that the woman brought up the issue of worship because Jesus' questions had become way too personal and much too difficult to answer.

What does worship mean to you? Write your understanding below and then consider how much your personal preferences influence your understanding. Does your personal preference make you take a side in worship disagreements? Can worship struggles impact the way individuals or a congregation understands God? Why?

PRAYER

"I love You, Lord, and I lift my voice in praise." Help me recognize all that can mean. Help me learn how to worship you through all things. Amen.

_____

_____

_____

_____

LIVING IN WORSHIP
Week 4: *The Ever-Present Spirit*
NOT TIED TO PLACE
John 4:21

"Woman," Jesus replied, "believe me, a time is coming when you will worship the Father neither on this mountain nor in Jerusalem."

One of my favorite places in Jerusalem is known as the Western Wall or the Wailing Wall. It is the believed to be the western edge of the original Temple mount, and it's the place Jews gather to pray, celebrate, study, and worship. In fact, Jews believed that the presence of God resided in the Temple. The last Temple was destroyed in A.D. 70 and the Western Wall represents the closest place Jews can get to the original Temple. It is a most sacred place for them.

Jesus understood the importance of the Temple to Jews. But He also knew that His mission on earth would change everything the Jews and the Samaritans believed about the importance of where they worshiped. In Matthew 16, Jesus revealed to His disciples that He was the Messiah and explained that His church would not be one built of stones but within the hearts and lives of His disciples.

Is your worship confined to place? In other words, do you worship wherever you are, or do you reserve your times of worship in a church facility? Why does the location help or hinder your personal worship? Respond below.

PRAYER
God, remind me that worship is meant to be a constant part of my life — not limited to a time or place. Help me become aware of You in such a way that I can be in worship in every action of my life. Amen.

LIVING IN WORSHIP
Week 4: *The Ever-Present Spirit*

WHO DO YOU WORSHIP? John 4:22

You Samaritans worship what you do not know; we worship what we do know, for salvation is from the Jews.

I recently had a conversation with an older adult who kept telling me about what "his God" would do or not do. The interesting thing was that his understanding of God was not based on his study of the Scripture, but on the way he thought "his God" would respond in any given situation. It can be a real temptation to try to make our understanding of God fit what we want Him to be, even to pick and chose the things we like about God.

Jesus confronted the Samaritan woman with a similar issue. When Israel fell to the Assyrians in 722 B.C., part of the kingdom was exiled. The remaining inhabitants intermarried with non-Jews, resulting in an intermingling of cultures and religious beliefs. At the time of Jesus, this "mixed" culture of Samaritans had its own temple and was despised by Jews for their compromise. Full of grace, Jesus clarified that culture and personal preference do not determine what is true about God.

Who is God? Are there ways that you have allowed your personal preferences or understanding influence who God is to you? If you discussed your understanding of God with four other people, would they challenge your assumptions? Is your understanding of God based on what you have read, heard, and studied? Why? Respond below.

PRAYER
"God of grace and God of glory...grant us wisdom, grant us courage for the living of these days." Grant me the wisdom to see who You are and the courage to accept You as You are. Amen.

_____

_____

_____

_____

_____

mathetes: THE MAKING OF A DISCIPLE

LIVING IN WORSHIP
Week 4: *The Ever-Present Spirit*
GOD IS SPIRIT
John 4:23–24

Yet a time is coming and has now come when the true worshipers will worship the Father in the Spirit and in truth, for they are the kind of worshipers the Father seeks. God is spirit, and his worshipers must worship in the Spirit and in truth.

My wife's sister has been researching their ancestors. She constantly uncovers another person in the family tree and with that discovery comes new understanding of how the experiences of the past has impacted their entire family. It can be easy to focus on the present without realizing how the past has influenced it. Ancestry.com has become an avenue for those who want to search the complexity of their background to understand their present in a new way.

In His conversation with the Samaritan woman, Jesus moved past the idea of where to worship to the One to be worshiped and described Him as "God is Spirit." Three other "God is" statements are used in the New Testament: God is light; God is love; and God is a consuming fire. All four of these reflect God's intangible nature. Often, we grab hold of the idea that we are made in God's image and want to picture Him as a material being that looks like us and acts like us—a being that is understandable in our tangible, human brains. Jesus' words remind us that God is so much more than we are—we can only begin to grasp the complexity and greatness of our God.

Reflect on the four "God is" statements above. How do these help you understand the Lord? Use a Bible dictionary or the concordance in your Bible to research these four statements. Then, write below your understanding of the complexity of God based on your study. Then use the adapted words of Psalm 24:10 below to guide your prayer.

PRAYER
Lord, help me be able to answer the psalmist's question in Spirit and in truth: Who is He, this King of glory? The Lord Almighty—He is the King of glory. Amen.

LIVING IN WORSHIP
Week 4: *The Ever-Present Spirit*

I AM HE   John 4:25–26

The woman said, "I know that Messiah" (called Christ) "is coming. When he comes, he will explain everything to us." Then Jesus declared, "I, the one speaking to you—I am he."

Our grandson is mildly autistic. He's bright, articulate, engaging, and entertaining. He's definitely one of a kind. One of the first things he learned was who he is...his name, his identity, and where he's from. He will walk up to strangers and introduce himself with his full name and where he's from. He knows who he is.

Jesus didn't often share His complete identity voluntarily, but He did with this Samaritan woman. I wonder why. Scholars propose that it was because it was early in His ministry and He wasn't well known at the time, or that because He was in Samaria, His declaration would be understood as religious and not political. I can't help but wonder if it was because He met that Samaritan woman where she was spiritually and was willing to expose Himself in order to reach her. Isn't that what He ultimately did for each of us? He exposed Himself to ridicule and torture and humiliation to the point of death for us. I can't believe that He would not have done what was necessary to reach the Samaritan woman as well.

Read the response of the Samaritan woman to Jesus' declaration in John 4:39-42. Notice that not only did she believe, but she immediately shared her experience with those in her town, even those who had once shunned her. And their response was to believe as well. Is that not a true act of worship? Below, remember how you met Jesus and record how you've shared that understanding with others. Was it an act of worship? Why?

PRAYER
Father God, You love me. You love me so much that You sent Your Son for me. Thank You for that gift of love, and grace, and salvation through Your Son. Amen.

_____

_____

_____

LIVING IN WORSHIP
Week 5: *Sacrificial Worship*
RECEIVING MERCY
Romans 11:30–32

Just as you who were at one time disobedient to God have now received mercy as a result of their disobedience, so they too have now become disobedient in order that they too may now receive mercy as a result of God's mercy to you. For God has bound everyone over to disobedience so that he may have mercy on them all.

So often, we evaluate ourselves by comparing ourselves to others. Are we thinner, faster, richer, stronger, smarter, better looking, more talented...the possibilities are endless. And if we're honest with ourselves, we can easily fall into that trap about our involvement as Christians. The danger comes in comparing ourselves in such a way that we become puffed up with pride over our status in Christ.

Paul wrote to a group of Christians who were former Gentiles living in Rome who had a tendency to compare themselves to Jewish Christians. These Gentile Christians had come into the faith without all the baggage, the rules, the regulations—the Law—the Jews had as a part of their understanding. It was easy for them to think that the grace they had received was more special than what had been given to the Jews. Paul reminded them that even though the Jews had had a special relationship with God for a long time, they had still been disobedient. His point to the Gentile Christians was to be careful, or they could easily fall into disobedience as well.

God's grace is given to all of us. We cannot earn it and we will never deserve it. How could you explain that grace to a non-believer? Record your response below. Then, prayerfully consider: Are you ever guilty of comparing your faith to someone else's in order to make you feel better? Why?

PRAYER
Our Father, You are full of grace and mercy that is available to all people. Help me accept Your grace whole-heartedly and to recognize how Your grace to all people is complete. Amen.

_____

_____

_____

_____

LIVING IN WORSHIP
Week 5: *Sacrificial Worship*

GOD'S UNREACHABLE DEPTHS — Romans 11:33

Oh, the depth of the riches of the wisdom and knowledge of God! How unsearchable his judgments, and his paths beyond tracing out!

The deepest place in any ocean on the world is the Challenger Deep in the Mariana Trench, which is almost 7 miles below the water's surface. Only three individuals have ever been able to reach its depths, two in 1960 and one in 2012, and only with the help of sophisticated dive equipment. Without those, this area would have remained unreachable. The word *unreachable* is seldom used in the world today. We've become used to exploring the depths of the seas and the far reaches of outer space.

The fact that something is reachable makes it finite...it has limits that can be photographed and explored. It can be approached and understood. Yet the depth of who God is, and all that He is, is beyond our finite minds. We cannot explore the depth of God's wisdom and knowledge, or of His mercy and grace. We will never fully know who God is. But He totally knows us!

The depth of God's wisdom, knowledge, judgment, and grace are beyond the reach of disobedient and sinful man. Yet, He reaches to us, closing the distance that we cannot navigate on our own. Prayerfully consider what that means to you, and journal your thoughts below.

PRAYER
God, You are beyond my understanding, and beyond my reach. Thank You for crossing that distance to make me Yours. Amen.

LIVING IN WORSHIP
Week 5: *Sacrificial Worship*

UNSOLICITED ADVICE Romans 11:34-35

Who has known the mind of the Lord? Or who has been his counselor? Who has ever given to God, that God should repay them?

Don't we all hate being around the person who knows everything and doesn't hesitate to tell us what we should or should not do? So often, that unsolicited advice is not based on knowledge of the situation or the people involved or even in past experiences for those involved. It's faulty advice at best.

Imagine, then, giving God unsolicited advice or telling Him what He needs to do, based on human understanding. When we remember the depths of His knowledge and His wisdom that we considered yesterday, it becomes obvious how ridiculous any advice from us to God would be. That's Paul's point...God is so far beyond our understanding that we would be foolish to think we can understand everything about Him, much less try to tell Him what to do. When Paul considered these characteristics of God, he responded in a doxology of praise (vv. 33-36).

Meditate on the depth of God's wisdom, His knowledge, His grace, and His mercy. Below, create your own doxology of praise for God, focusing on these characteristics.

PRAYER
God, I am nothing compared to You. Yet, You love me...completely and in spite of who I am and all that I do that brings You dishonor. Help me to bring only honor to You, because You deserve nothing else. Amen.

LIVING IN WORSHIP
Week 5: *Sacrificial Worship*
A LIVING SACRIFICE Romans 12:1

Therefore, I urge you, brothers and sisters, in view of God's mercy, to offer your bodies as a living sacrifice, holy and pleasing to God—this is your true and proper worship.

Some things don't come naturally. I love to run and do it almost daily. But when I tried to run a marathon years ago, I understood that the distance of 26.2 miles didn't come naturally. There's a reason many runners rely on the encouragement of those on the sidelines to complete a race. The encouragers on the sideline are just urging the runners on, helping them accomplish what they've already committed to do.

Paul used the word "urge" to encourage his readers to do what they already knew they were to do. For Paul, the consummate teacher, to use the word "urge" demonstrates how well he understood his audience. He couldn't command them or force them to do what was expected of them. And that expectation involved worship as the first priority in a believer's life. That worship involves a lifestyle in which a believer's very life becomes his or her testimony of worship.

Below, describe what it means for your life to be a living sacrifice in worship of God. Then, evaluate your statement: Is it an accurate reflection of your life? Are you pleased with that description? Would others recognize your life as "a living sacrifice"? Why?

PRAYER
Father God, I offer my life to You as a living sacrifice. Teach me how to let my life belong totally to You. Amen.

_____

_____

_____

_____

_____

LIVING IN WORSHIP
Week 5: *Sacrificial Worship*

BE TRANSFORMED
Romans 12:2

Do not conform to the pattern of this world, but be transformed by the renewing of your mind. Then you will be able to test and approve what God's will is—his good, pleasing and perfect will.

Our son pledged a fraternity while in college. We watched him become like his fraternity brothers as he conformed to the required dress code and acted within the rules of the fraternity. As we watched, we saw both positives and negatives in his conformity. However, while the outward appearance may have changed, inside he remained the same kid he had always been. There was no long-term transformation of his life.

Paul urged his readers to not just change the way they looked or acted, but to be transformed into a new creature in Christ. The definition of the word "transformation" includes having a marked change. Paul described that change in spiritual terms. As we are transformed into disciples, we will gain the spiritual discernment to understand God's will. That is a picture of true transformation.

In the area below, use these questions to evaluate your own transformation: How is your life different today than it was as a new believer? Than it was before you were a believer? Do you recognize God's transformation in your life? What areas in your life do you see God transforming at this time?

PRAYER
God, help me to know You deeper daily. Help me to know Your thoughts and Your will in my life. And help me become totally transformed into what You would have me to be. Amen.

LIVING IN WORSHIP
Week 6: *Worship is Forever*
IMAGINING HEAVEN
Revelation 4:6-8

Also in front of the throne there was what looked like a sea of glass, clear as crystal. In the center, around the throne, were four living creatures, and they were covered with eyes, in front and in back. The first living creature was like a lion, the second was like an ox, the third had a face like a man, the fourth was like a flying eagle. Each of the four living creatures had six wings and was covered with eyes all around, even under its wings. Day and night they never stop saying: 'Holy, holy, holy is the Lord God Almighty,' who was, and is, and is to come."

Both my wife and I have experienced the loss of a parent. As we worked through the grieving process, we couldn't help but wonder what our dads were experiencing. We drew comfort in knowing where they were and with whom. But what could that experience be like? John's vision of heaven can help us visualize what that experience will one day be like for us as well.

In the fourth chapter of Revelation, John experienced a vision that actually transported him to heaven. There, he witnessed first-hand the glory of God's presence and the eternal praise that was given Him. When we arrive in heaven, God and all His glory will be revealed totally to us. At that moment, we will understand completely what it means to worship the Holy God.

Notice the final words in this passage that describe God: "who was, and is, and is to come." He always was involved in His world, is still, and always will be. In all that time, He was, is, and remains holy. Focus on the thought that your God is holy and then record what that means to you personally. Could you worship an unholy God? Why not?

PRAYER
Holy, holy, holy God, You alone know what it means to be Holy. You alone are holy. You alone can teach me how to be holy. Teach me, Lord, so I can praise You in Your holiness. Amen.

_____

_____

_____

_____

36 mathetes: THE MAKING OF A DISCIPLE

LIVING IN WORSHIP
Week 6: *Worship is Forever*
BEING WORTHY
Revelation 4:9-11

Whenever the living creatures give glory, honor and thanks to him who sits on the throne and who lives forever and ever, the twenty-four elders fall down before him who sits on the throne and worship him who lives forever and ever. They lay their crowns before the throne and say: "You are worthy, our Lord and God, to receive glory and honor and power, for you created all things, and by your will they were created and have their being."

We arrived late at a training conference and had to squeeze into the back of a balcony at a large church. Having driven over four hours in heavy traffic to get there, I wasn't that thrilled to sit through another long, general session. However, the choir began a piece that praised God through just reciting the names of God. As the choir sang, people started parading up and down the aisles with banners proclaiming God's names. As each name was added, the people in the audience began to rise spontaneously to their feet to worship God aloud as well. By the time the choir finished, the entire sanctuary had erupted in worship and praise. I had never experienced anything like that before. I witnessed a holy moment.

John described an event somewhat like the one I experienced as he continued to share his vision in chapter 4. In verse 8, the four creatures around the throne of God praised God continually day and night. In verse 9, the twenty-four elders put their crowns on God's throne and joined the praise. Because of that worship experience I had, I can imagine the growing cacophony of sound as the praises rose above God's throne. John witnessed a holy moment.

Have you witnessed and participated in such a holy moment? If not, what would you expect such a holy moment to be like? Respond below.

PRAYER
God, You are holy and You are worthy. Help me recognize Your power over all things and the glory that can only belong to You. Amen.

_____

_____

_____

_____

LIVING IN WORSHIP
Week 6: *Worship is Forever*

ONE IN THE CROWD
Revelation 7:9

After this I looked, and there before me was a great multitude that no one could count, from every nation, tribe, people and language, standing before the throne and before the Lamb. They were wearing white robes and were holding palm branches in their hands.

Our daughter is not a big fan of crowds. The bigger the crowd, the more anxious she gets. For many of us, though, big noisy crowds indicate something important that has drawn thousands of people together—like the Super Bowl, or the Final Four, or a Christmas parade, or shopping the day after Thanksgiving. In these crowds, you'd be hard pressed to find something all those gathered could agree upon.

In his vision, John saw a crowd that was too large to be counted but shared one common purpose—to praise God. In the story of the Tower of Babel in Genesis, God separated mankind by hindering their ability to communicate as His judgment for them trying to reach heaven on their own. John saw a time when mankind came together, from every nation and every language, as one. And they came humbly before God, recognizing that there is only God, and that no other creature can take His place.

There are many scholarly opinions about these people clothed in white robes. Many believe they were martyred for their faith in God. Whatever their faith experience, they had become part of the universal chorus of praise for God. It is a picture of worship and true peace. What does that moment suggest to you about eternal life? How would you share your understanding with a non-believer? Respond below.

PRAYER
Lord, help me become part of that universal chorus of praise. Help me be a witness also of Your peace to all people. Amen.

LIVING IN WORSHIP
Week 6: *Worship is Forever*
BEING SAVED
Revelation 7:10

And they cried out in a loud voice: "Salvation belongs to our God, who sits on the throne, and to the Lamb."

Our son is a firefighter and an EMT. Recently, he was eating lunch with his family when another customer's defibrillator went off. Scott jumped up to help, rendered immediate first aid, and was on the phone with the 911-operator when the man stopped breathing completely. Within a couple of seconds, Scott started compression on the man's chest. In less than a minute, the man began to breath again. Obviously, the man's family was grateful for Scott's actions in saving the life of their dad. But Scott's actions can only be temporary. That man and all us of will eventually leave this life behind.

As John watched the scene before him, he heard the next set of praises as the gathered multitude acknowledged that salvation—eternal salvation—can only come through God on His throne and through His Son. In that picture of heaven, John was able to see the completion of God's plan for His people. They could come before Him in praise at the final conclusion of His plan, when His Kingdom in heaven has been victorious over sin.

When Jesus died for us, it was a once-for-all action and it covers us into eternity. Consider how that act influences your worship of God. Below, create your prayer of thanksgiving and praise for the salvation God has provided for you.

PRAYER
Lord, thank You for Your saving grace, for loving me so much that You were willing to send Your Son to do what I could not do for myself. Please don't allow me to ever forget what You've done for me. Amen.

_____

_____

_____

_____

_____

LIVING IN WORSHIP
Week 6: *Worship is Forever*

ETERNAL PRAISE
Revelation 7:11–12

All the angels were standing around the throne and around the elders and the four living creatures. They fell down on their faces before the throne and worshiped God, saying: "Amen! Praise and glory and wisdom and thanks and honor and power and strength be to our God for ever and ever. Amen!"

We live on about one hundred acres of land that my grandfather bought in the early 1930s. Within a few years, he built a small house on the property and started a garden. The family has been planted here ever since. After my grandparents passed away, the property was passed on to my father. When he died a few years ago, the property came to me. And there will be a time when the land will be passed down to my son and then to his son. It's become a family legacy. As far as I can see into the future, our family will shoulder the responsibility of serving as stewards of this land and this heritage. It is as close to having something eternal in this lifetime as I will ever know.

Worship is the true eternal act. As John saw in his vision, the creatures at the throne, the elders, and the gathered multitudes fell on their faces in worship before the one and only holy God. The picture of lying prostrate on the ground indicates the level of humility and worship. Remember the story in Daniel when Shadrach, Meshach, and Abednego, were required to fall on the ground in worship of a statue of the king? They refused because only the Lord God Almighty was worthy of that level of worship. In these verses, John saw true worship before God and heard the worshipers praising God.

The words in verse 12 have been described as seven doxologies offered to God: *praise, glory, wisdom, thanks, honor, power,* and *strength*. Each word describes how we worship God and each reflects who He is. Meditate on the meaning of each of these words and then write in the space provided a statement of prayer for each one.

PRAYER
Father God, You are God and You are worthy of my praise and adoration and thanks. May Your name be glorified in all I do. And may I never forget all that You are in my life. Amen.

_____

_____

_____

UNDERTAKING HOLY DISCIPLINES
Week 7: *The Discipline of Prayer*

HUNGRY FOR POWER — Luke 11:1

One day Jesus was praying in a certain place. When he finished, one of his disciples said to him, "Lord, teach us to pray, just as John taught his disciples."

Where Jesus was when He taught his disciples how to pray isn't recorded in Luke's gospel. What is recorded is what prompted the conversation—a disciple who watched and heard Jesus pray suddenly recognized the inadequacy of his own prayers. A hunger was awakened in him. "Teach us to pray," he asked Jesus.

How moving it must have been to hear the Son of God pray. To witness the communion Jesus had with God the Father must have stirred in the disciple a longing to know and experience real prayer. How different we would be if we were hungry for prayer.

Ask God today to show you the significance of time in prayer and time spent with Him. How important is prayer to you? Ask God to remind you of prayers He has answered. Ask God to teach you how to pray.

PRAYER
Heavenly Father, give me a hunger for prayer and a desire to know You better. Teach me to pray. Amen.

UNDERTAKING HOLY DISCIPLINES
Week 7: *The Discipline of Prayer*

PERFECT TIMING — Luke 11:3

Give us each day our daily bread.

The writing assignment for my denomination's national news service was, in some ways, the most important assignment I'd ever received. I was honored to join the month-long project. I needed to give it my best.

Writing vignettes on missions meant phone calls to pastors across the nation. Caught between pastors' busy schedules and hard deadlines, stress mounted as I found myself continually racing against the clock. One morning, I read a missionary's story of near calamity in my daily devotional guide. Panic had threatened to overtake the missionary until she realized God was at work "even when the clock was ticking."

Trusting God for a writing deadline seemed trivial compared to the missionary's predicament. Still, I began to relax. Over the next three weeks, I marveled as God brought me exactly what I needed for that day's article, and nothing more. As I committed daily to depend on Him, He showed me His faithfulness.

Do you struggle to trust God for today? Use the space below to list your needs as you commit them to God.

PRAYER

Heavenly Father, help me to depend on You daily. Help me remember that You are at work to provide for my every need even if I don't see it. Amen.

UNDERTAKING HOLY DISCIPLINES
Week 7: *The Discipline of Prayer*

THE SCANDAL OF FORGIVENESS — Luke 11:4

Forgive us our sins, for we also forgive everyone who sins against us. And lead us not into temptation.

Forgiveness is hard. Sometimes it seems scandalous. Wisconsin minister Roy Ratcliff witnessed a change in convicted serial killer and cannibal Jeffrey Dahmer after his confession of faith in Christ. Ratcliff was dismayed to discover that fellow believers found Dahmer's claim to forgiveness hard to accept.

Forgiveness is costly. The great devotional writer Oswald Chambers cautioned against preaching forgiveness as simply an outpouring of God's love. Chambers wrote that to do so would trivialize the costly redemption Christ won for us on the cross: "God could forgive men in no other way than by the death of His Son."

Only when we understand the severity and depth of sin can we truly appreciate what Christ accomplished. Only when we understand the price that was paid can we extend forgiveness to others.

What sin do you need to confess? Whom do you need to forgive? Use the space below to consider the wrongs you need to confess. List the names of those whom you need to forgive.

PRAYER
Heavenly Father, thank You for Your incredible gift of forgiveness. Help me to understand the price Jesus paid for my sin. Help me to forgive others. Amen.

UNDERTAKING HOLY DISCIPLINES
Week 7: *The Discipline of Prayer*
PRAY LIKE A SALESMAN
Luke 11:9

So I say to you: Ask and it will be given to you; seek and you will find; knock and the door will be opened to you.

In his book *Prayer: Does It Make Any Difference?*, Philip Yancey writes, "We should pray like a salesman with his foot wedged in the door opening, like a wrestler who has his opponent in a headlock and won't let go." Heaven welcomes persistence.

In Luke chapter 11, wedged in-between the familiar Lord's Prayer and this verse, Jesus told the story of the cranky neighbor who finally roused from slumber to answer a friend's bold pleading for help. It's a scenario we understand: the complainer gets attention; the "squeaky wheel gets the oil." Jesus used the story to show us that God invites us to come to Him with every need, present every request, even "pound the doors of heaven."

When we ask first for God's will as the model prayer teaches, and persist in prayer as the parable demonstrates, He opens the vast resources of heaven to answer. What bold requests will you present to Him today?

PRAYER
Heavenly Father, teach us to pray first that Your will is done in every situation. You listen to every request. You answer the pleas of our hearts. Amen.

UNDERTAKING HOLY DISCIPLINES
Week 7: *The Discipline of Prayer*

THE MOST NEEDED GIFT
Luke 11:11-13

Which of you fathers, if your son asks for a fish, will give him a snake instead? Or if he asks for an egg, will give him a scorpion? If you then, though you are evil, know how to give good gifts to your children, how much more will your Father in heaven give the Holy Spirit to those who ask him!

What parent doesn't enjoy watching a child open a gift on Christmas morning? Few things in life are as satisfying as giving a loved one a long-wished-for present. In this passage, Jesus ended His instructions on prayer with a thrilling promise: God is willing and anxious to grant His children's requests.

Yet God is not content to give gifts that in the end do not satisfy. He longs to give us what we really need: we need Him. How freely He offers Himself to His children.

Do you seek God for His gifts or do you seek Him? In the space below, consider your typical requests to God. Reflect on what it means to seek Him rather than seeking His blessing.

PRAYER
Heavenly Father, help me to run to You with every care and concern. More importantly, help me to seek You rather than seeking Your blessing. Amen.

UNDERTAKING HOLY DISCIPLINES
Week 8: *The Discipline of Scripture Study*

A RELIABLE G.P.S. — Psalm 119:19

How can a young person stay on the path of purity? By living according to your word.

The tiny box in my car called a global positioning system insisted I turn left. Almost immediately, I knew my digital friend had steered me wrong. Instead of paved highway, I was traveling a dirt road. Instead of civilization, I was driving deeper into thick woods broken only by the occasional broken-down house or abandoned trailer.

Today's culture puts out signals that are slick and shiny and give every impression of being trustworthy. Only later do we discover that the directions we've been given have left us anxious, alone, and headed for danger.

In a world where wrong is called right, how do we find our way? Psalm 1 says that when God's Law is our "G.P.S.", we thrive and flourish. Contentment will be ours in abundance.

What signals from a secular world tend to trip you up? Are you tempted by material possessions? Money? Take a moment to jot down the things that divert your attention from God.

PRAYER
Heavenly Father, help me to guard my heart by studying and memorizing Your Word. Give me a love for Your Word that is fresh and fulfilling. Amen.

UNDERTAKING HOLY DISCIPLINES
Week 8: *The Discipline of Scripture Study*
A SHELTER AGAINST THE STORM Psalm 119:11

I have hidden your word in my heart; that I might not sin against you.

The days were hard. My faith was being tested. As I searched the Bible looking for direction, peace and comfort, Scripture came alive for me. I found Psalm 61 and was reminded of the countless times God had come to my rescue before.

Difficult days dragged into weeks, then months, but I carried Psalm 61:3 in my heart: "Lead me to the rock that is higher than I, for you have been my refuge, my strong tower against the enemy." I began to realize that I needed Him more than I needed relief from the problem. God used this passage and others to anchor my ever-so-weak faith and to keep me from being overwhelmed by waves of doubt and fear and falling into sin.

What daunting task is God asking you to do today? Is your trust in God faltering? Perhaps you now face a temptation to do something that would dishonor Him? Express your thoughts below on how Scripture can help you face this challenge.

PRAYER
Heavenly Father, help me to carry Your Word in my heart. Use Your Scripture to tune my heart to Yours and keep me from doubt and disobedience. Amen.

Week 8: *The Discipline of Scripture Study*

A FAILED MYTH — Psalm 119:12

Praise be to you, LORD; teach me your decrees.

"Humans should pursue honesty, justice, industry and charity for all." Sounds almost biblical, doesn't it? Though humanism embraces values that sound similar to Christian virtues, humanism at its core falls far short of what Scripture teaches about humankind.

Scripture says we are valuable to God because He created us; sin has corrupted our human nature and our world. Humanism, at the opposite pole, rejects God and sees human beings as intrinsically good. The problem for humanism then is, as R. C. Sproul wrote, "The standard of 'goodness' must be low enough that the average person can meet it consistently." The myth of human goodness fails as the world sinks deeper into decay.

Who are we? How did we get here? Is it possible to live lives that are pleasing to God? Studying God's Word will give us the direction we need in a world that has turned its back on its Creator.

Prayerfully consider the Scripture verse(s) you want to memorize at this point in your spiritual journey. Use the space below to jot down that reference. Practice repeating the verse(s) from memory this week.

PRAYER
Heavenly Father, teach me Your ways. Give me a hunger and a love for Your Word. Amen.

UNDERTAKING HOLY DISCIPLINES
Week 8: *The Discipline of Scripture Study*

BETTER THAN RICHES — Psalm 119:14

I rejoice in following your statutes as one rejoices in great riches.

Much of the literary beauty and complexity of Psalm 119 is lost when translated into English. The twenty-two stanzas that make up the psalm are an alphabetical acrostic, each ticking off the next letter in the Hebrew alphabet. Even the eight verses within each stanza begin with the same Hebrew letter, something the English reader won't see.

The beautiful structure of the psalm communicates the psalmist's conviction that God's Law is both deeply satisfying and more valuable than riches. In contrast, the world offers wealth, recognition, and comfort that leave us empty. As Elizabeth Elliott wrote in *Keep a Quiet Heart*, "Things we feel sure we need for happiness may often lead to our ruin." Psalm 119 is a testimony to the satisfying richness and timelessness of God's Law.

What do you pursue? Do you spend more time with a favorite hobby than you do with Scripture? Does your career consume you? Use the space below to write about something that once consumed you but is now no longer important. Explain why.

PRAYER
Heavenly Father, give me a love for Your Law. Help me to discover its incredible wealth and find its deepest treasures. Amen.

UNDERTAKING HOLY DISCIPLINES
Week 8: The Discipline of Scripture Study

AN ANTI-VIRUS FOR ATTACK

Psalm 119:15-16

I meditate on your precepts and consider your ways. I delight in your decrees; I will not neglect your word.

To change a culture, start with a child. Richard Dawkins, a New Atheist known for vitriolic attacks on religion, wrote a children's book meant to make Christianity look like an outdated myth. Foes of traditional marriage have made inroads into the culture by winning over today's youth.

Detractors often attack a mere caricature of the faith. Christians are labeled as ignorant, weak, deluded "sheep" who follow blindly after a fairy tale. Christians must respond in grace with well-reasoned Scriptural answers and from the wealth of material that undergirds our understanding of faith.

The best anti-virus against attacks on faith is a deep commitment to the study of God's Word. 1 Peter 3:15 urges us to be prepared "to give an answer to everyone who asks you to give the reason for the hope that you have."

Can you name the writer, setting, audience, and major themes of a single book in the Bible? Jot down below everything you know about one book of the Bible. Would you be able to use this knowledge to support your faith to a non-believer? Commit to learning more as a part of your spiritual journey.

PRAYER

Heavenly Father, help me be a student of Your Word. Lead me as I discover the richness of Scripture. Amen.

UNDERTAKING HOLY DISCIPLINES
Week 9: *The Discipline of Fasting*
NO TURNING BACK   Matthew 4:1

Then Jesus was led by the Spirit into the wilderness to be tempted by the devil.

The significance of Jesus being led into the desert to be tempted is not small. His mission was confirmed at His baptism. His ministry was about to begin.

This passage makes the promise of Hebrews 4:15 that our High Priest "was tempted in every way, just as we are" meaningful. Jesus resisted using His supernatural resources to serve Himself. N.T. Wright, in part one of his *Matthew for Everyone* commentary, wrote this about the significance of Jesus' response to being tempted: "He is committed to living off God's word; to trusting God completely, without setting up trick tests to put God on the spot. He is committed to loving and serving God alone" (p. 25).

This is what fasting is meant to be—we reign in some small part of our lives, for some brief period, as a statement of our commitment to Him. By God's grace, we don't give in to fleshly indulgences. By His grace, we don't turn back.

Ask God to show you how and when you should fast. Write out your thoughts on how fasting will help you focus on Him.

PRAYER
Heavenly Father, I want to give You control over every part of my life. Teach me about fasting. Amen.

UNDERTAKING HOLY DISCIPLINES
Week 9: *The Discipline of Fasting*

A CHANGED FOCUS — Matthew 4:2

After fasting forty days and forty nights, he was hungry.

In C. S. Lewis' *The Chronicles of Narnia: Prince Caspian*, Lucy found herself irritated and anxious to tell her older sister exactly what she thought. Her frustrated thoughts melted away when Aslan, the Christ-figure of the novel series, came near. Lewis wrote, "She forgot them when she fixed her eyes on Aslan."

When we fix our eyes on Christ and train our focus on Him, the petty grievances and cares of our sin-weary world shrink into the background. Fasting is not meant to be a ritual we feel obligated to do, but a release as we run into His arms. As we come to Christ seeking direction, cleansing from sin, help for someone in need, or a deeper communion with Him, our daily physical needs don't disappear, but they do pale in comparison.

Is there a need pressing on your heart? Have you placed it in His hands? Use the space below to reflect on what God is calling you to do in regards to fasting.

PRAYER
Heavenly Father, help me to focus on You completely. Help me to approach fasting as You intended it to be. Amen.

UNDERTAKING HOLY DISCIPLINES
Week 9: *The Discipline of Fasting*

ENTANGLED
Matthew 4:1-2

Then Jesus was led by the Spirit into the wilderness to be tempted by the devil. After fasting forty days and forty nights, he was hungry.

A friend once quipped as we departed on yet another shoe shopping spree, "It's not about need. It's about greed." We laughed, knowing we both had a closet full of shoes but were willing to make room for one more pair.

Clearly, my friend and I had ignored Paul's admonition in Romans 13:14 about giving in to the desires of a sinful nature. Paul did not give a prohibition against caring for one's needs, but instead warned against indulging selfish desires and lusts. Mike Aquilina, in *A Year With the Church Fathers*, included this comment from fifth-century monk St. John Cassian: "[Paul] does not want us to pamper the flesh, and end up dangerously tangled in its desires" (p. 270).

Fasting is a way to free oneself from the entanglements of the world and an indulgent focus on self. Use the space below to list things, possessions, or desires that interfere with a whole-hearted commitment to God. Then, prayerfully consider what God would have you change in the way you approach your possessions and your desires.

PRAYER
Heavenly Father, show me the things I have let take Your place. Bring my focus back to You, and You alone. Amen.

UNDERTAKING HOLY DISCIPLINES
Week 9: *The Discipline of Fasting*
A PATH OF FREEDOM   Matthew 4:1

Then Jesus was led by the Spirit into the wilderness to be tempted by the devil.

As German pastor Dietrich Bonhoeffer penned the words to *The Cost of Discipleship*, his homeland was falling under the spell of Hitler's godless regime. For Bonhoeffer, the price for being an outspoken follower of Christ would mean imprisonment and execution just days before Allied troops brought liberation.

Bonhoeffer wrote this: "Fasting helps to discipline the self-indulgent and slothful will which is so reluctant to serve the Lord." Only in a disciplined life can "the flesh learn the painful lesson that it has no rights of its own" (pp. 188-9).

Biographer Eric Metaxas concluded that Bonhoeffer was not advocating a sparse, ascetic life for Christians away from the world. Rather, Bonhoeffer saw discipline as a pathway to freedom and the Christian faith as the "means to live life more fully" (*Bonhoeffer*, pp. 484-5). True freedom is a life lived unshackled by sin.

Jesus prepared for ministry by fasting in the desert. What service is God calling you to? Are you prepared for the path ahead? Respond to these questions below.

PRAYER
Heavenly Father, I give You my life. Bring my will and my nature under Your control. Make me useable for service. Then, may I know Your joy. Amen.

UNDERTAKING HOLY DISCIPLINES
Week 9: *The Discipline of Fasting*

FREED TO WORSHIP
Matthew 4:4

Jesus answered, "It is written: 'Man does not live on bread alone, but on every word that comes from the mouth of God.'"

Fasting is only good if it frees a believer to spend time with God. Fasting done so a checkmark can be made on a spiritual checklist or so God will know "I really mean this prayer this time" will only bring frustration and emptiness.

A growing Christian who prays will begin to understand that to talk to God means more than having wishes granted and requests answered. Likewise, fasting should bring us into His presence and free us to worship Him. When we leave, we should feel refreshed.

In his book *Worship is a Verb*, Robert E. Webber writes: "I find myself deeply moved in reverence and humility whenever I realize that in worship I am responding to the almighty and ever-living God who is transcendent, the God who pervades the limitless universe" (p. 110).

Do you look forward to spending time with God? Or, are you hoping that fasting will "convince" God to grant your request? Reflect below on your motivation for fasting.

PRAYER
Heavenly Father, teach me the purpose of fasting. Help me to embrace it as a time of sweet communion with You. Amen.

UNDERTAKING HOLY DISCIPLINES
Week 10: *The Discipline of Giving*

EVERYTHING — Mark 12:41

Jesus sat down opposite the place where the offerings were put and watched the crowd putting their money into the temple treasury. Many rich people threw in large amounts.

A college student queried a Christian speaker about the Old Testament instruction to tithe: Was it ten percent? Are believers bound to Old Testament directives? Isn't it legalistic to expect Christians to abide by guidelines that pre-date Christ? The speaker gave this response: "Why don't you give what the blood of Christ is worth to you?"

His point hits home. No gift, no offering, could ever match what Christ accomplished on the Cross. The redemption He won replaces old broken lives with new ones. He breathes value and hope and joy into lives tossed aside by the world like old pairs of shoes.

How would you act if you knew Jesus was watching as you put your offering in the collection plate? Do your gifts reflect the value of Christ's sacrifice? List below the blessings God has given you. How does your giving compare?

PRAYER
Heavenly Father, help me to realize how wide and long and high and deep Your love is. Give me a heart of gratitude for all You have done. Amen.

UNDERTAKING HOLY DISCIPLINES
Week 10: *The Discipline of Giving*

A MATTER OF THE HEART Mark 12:42

But a poor widow came and put in two very small copper coins, worth only a few cents.

Ed could be counted on to make a contribution whenever a need arose. When someone in the church needed help, Ed would give. Once, when it became apparent that the church would be forced to replace some office equipment, Ed stood up and announced he would give the first hundred dollars. His giving was impressive. That is, until it became known that Ed didn't give to the church budget. Ed liked to give when others would notice.

The widow's two coins made little noise when they fell into the temple's trumpet-shaped receptacles. Only Jesus noticed. 1 Samuel 16:7 reminds us that "man looks at the outward appearance, but the Lord looks at the heart."

Do you give beyond what you can afford to spare? Do you give or serve others hoping someone will notice? Below, compare what you give to what you own. How do they compare?

PRAYER
Heavenly Father, change my heart and make me willing to give You everything I own. Show me what you want me to give. Amen.

UNDERTAKING HOLY DISCIPLINES
Week 10: *The Discipline of Giving*

NICKELS AND DIMES — Mark 12:42

But a poor widow came and put in two very small copper coins, worth only a few cents.

My husband had taken a new job and we were living on a reduced budget when my eleven-year-old daughter approached me with a request. She wanted to open a lemonade stand to "raise money for camp."

Pleased that my young daughter wanted to help with the expense of sending three of us to church camp—herself, her younger sister, and me as a counselor—I agreed. How surprised I was when two weeks later she had raised more than one hundred-eighty dollars. How ashamed I was when I realized I had completely misunderstood. The money was not for us; the money would pay an unchurched friend's way to camp. I was consumed with dollars and cents. She was focused on things of eternal value. I believe the nickels and dimes she collected to help a friend learn about Jesus pleased Him more than all my offerings combined.

Write down in the space below areas where you spend your money. Write beside it whether it is an investment with an eternal value.

PRAYER
Heavenly Father, forgive me for holding back. Teach me that everything I own comes from Your hand. Amen.

UNDERTAKING HOLY DISCIPLINES
Week 10: *The Discipline of Giving*
UNBOUNDED WEALTH
Mark 12:44

They all gave out of their wealth; but she, out of her poverty...

Ann became a widow for the second time when her husband was murdered. Both of her young adult sons were mentally handicapped; her only daughter battled a serious illness. However, to say that Ann was poor would be to describe her as others count wealth. For when it came to a gentle and caring spirit, Ann was fabulously wealthy.

Regularly and generously, Ann brought gifts to others. Sometimes it was a picture one of her sons had drawn with crayons. Other times it was beans from her garden she'd canned herself or a small craft she made from clothespins and yarn. Each time I accepted one of Ann's gifts, I was reminded that I gave out of abundance. She gave sacrificially.

Ann never complained, never questioned God, never bemoaned what life had dealt her. She was boundlessly happy and contented. Joy was truly hers.

How is your giving? Do you hold back because you are worried about bills? Debt? Retirement? Use the space below to list possessions that are not truly necessities. Ask God what you should do with each.

PRAYER
Heavenly Father, show me my incredible wealth. Help me to let it go. Give me a heart of giving to others. Amen.

UNDERTAKING HOLY DISCIPLINES
Week 10: *The Discipline of Giving*

A COMMITMENT DARE Proverbs 3:9

Honor the Lord with your wealth, with the firstfruits of all your crops.

One of the hymns so familiar to yesterday's generation is one penned a century ago by Howard B. Grose: *Give of Your Best to the Master.* The words seem so timely for today's ever-darkening world that it's easy to forget that every generation of believers has been called to be a standard bearer for truth.

> *Give of your best to the Master;*
> *Give of the strength of your youth;*
> *Throw your soul's fresh, glowing ardor*
> *Into the battle for truth.*

Scripture makes it clear that God is concerned with how we spend our money. But commitment to God is much more than writing a tithe check. We must devote all of ourselves—our minds, our study, our passions—to Him. We must give Him our best.

How different would the world be if Christians devoted their thoughts and ability to learn to God? How different would your life be if you laid your time schedule, your work, your hobbies and your talents before Him? For this, we must. A desperate world is waiting. Below, record your responses to these questions. Then prayerfully mediate on this statement: A desperate world is waiting. What would God have you do?

PRAYER
Heavenly Father, help me to trust You enough to give You my very best. Lead me as I devote all to You. Amen.

UNDERTAKING HOLY DISCIPLINES
Week 11: *The Discipline of Meditation*

THE SANCTUARY
Philippians 4:5

The Lord is near.

God brought several opportunities to adopt into the lives of author and speaker Diane Nix and her pastor-husband, but each opportunity ended in agonizing disappointment. Then, the couple learned she was pregnant. One morning during her quiet time, Diane heard God ask her, "Did you give Me this child?"

Several days later, friends gathered in the hospital room as Diane delivered a stillborn baby girl, a beautiful "newborn-pink" from the oxygen given to Diane during delivery. During the long labor, Diane had focused on the 1 Samuel 1:2 passage she had taught in Bible Study the week before—Hannah's anguish before the Lord and her surrender of her son Samuel.

"The hospital room became a sanctuary," Diane said of that day. "It was an incredible time of God's presence." In the years that followed, the Lord blessed Diane and her husband with two healthy daughters.

Remembering Scripture can anchor our faith and bring peace though storms rage about us. Below, write your requests to God, remembering that He is faithful and can be trusted completely.

PRAYER
Heavenly Father, I am afraid and timid. Teach me Your Scripture so I can remember Your faithfulness, kindness, and incredible mercy. Amen.

UNDERTAKING HOLY DISCIPLINES
Week 11: *The Discipline of Meditation*

KEEPING THE PEACE

Philippians 4:6

Do not be anxious about anything, but in every situation, by prayer and petition, with thanksgiving, present your requests to God.

In *Keep a Quiet Heart*, Elizabeth Elliott wrote that hymns and spiritual songs have been invaluable to her in her spiritual development. Keeping Scripture ever present in our hearts and minds can keep our faith vibrant and our anxiety down.

Prayerlessness is the number one way to "forfeit the peace God wants us to have," Elliott wrote. But there are other ways: "resent God's ways; worry as much as possible; pray only about things you can't manage by yourself; refuse to accept what God gives; look for peace elsewhere than in Him; try to rule your own life; doubt God's word; carry all your cares" (p. 59).

God, who is rich in mercy, welcomes our every request. When we lay our requests at His feet, He gathers us in His arms and pulls us close. If we trust Him to answer in His infinite wisdom, peace will be ours in abundance.

Write in the space provided below any request pressing on your heart. When you finish, write this: "I give this to God. I trust Him with His answer."

PRAYER
Heavenly Father, I can't say thank You enough for all You've done. Help me to trust You more. Amen.

_____

_____

_____

_____

UNDERTAKING HOLY DISCIPLINES
Week 11: *The Discipline of Meditation*
PEACE AND PRESENCE OF MIND — Philippians 4:6

Do not be anxious about anything...

It's hard not to be anxious when the Christian faith is openly attacked. Richard Dawkins, former Oxford University professor and author of *The God Delusion*, encouraged a crowd of atheists at a 2012 gathering in Washington D. C. to aggressively confront people of faith. "Mock them," Dawkins told the crowd. "Ridicule them! In public!"

How do we face detractors who taunt us and misrepresent the faith? Only in laying our concerns before the Lord can we respond with gentleness (v. 5), find peace (v. 7), and have presence of mind enough to think clearly (v. 8).

Dawkins has credentials as a scientist and is a talented communicator, but his case against God falls flat. Christian scholarly responses are numerous and easy to find and understand. The thoughtful response that today's culture demands is something every Christian can be prepared to give.

The gospel is true, noble, right, pure, and lovely. Do you think about what you believe and why? Sketch out a plan below for how you can increase your knowledge of the gospel.

PRAYER
Heavenly Father, help me to be a better student of Your Word. Help me to respond calmly to those whose hearts are hard against You. Amen.

UNDERTAKING HOLY DISCIPLINES
Week 11: *The Discipline of Meditation*

THE UNGUARDED MIND
Philippians 4:8

Finally, brothers and sisters, whatever is true, whatever is noble, whatever is right, whatever is pure, whatever is lovely, whatever is admirable—if anything is excellent or praiseworthy—think about such things.

On the eve of his execution, serial murderer Ted Bundy requested an audience with Dr. James Dobson, Christian psychologist and founder of Focus on the Family. In the interview, Bundy identified pornography as the catalyst that started a chain reaction of sexual deviation, violence, and murder.

Bundy was raised in a Christian home but stumbled upon pornography as a boy. His story is one of a fast slide into an abyss he could not escape. He requested the interview for the sole purpose of warning others about the dangers of pornography. Of his fellow inmates imprisoned for violence, Bundy insisted each had a link to pornography.

Advertisers know we are persuaded by what we see. In today's technology-driven culture, guarding the mind is more important than ever. Meditating on Scripture can protect the mind and keep a believer focused on Christ. Below, sketch out how much time you spend in front of the television, computer, I-Pad, or other device. How much of what you see is dangerous to you?

PRAYER
Heavenly Father, keep my way pure. Help me to stay away from images that are harmful. Turn my focus to You. Amen.

UNDERTAKING HOLY DISCIPLINES
Week 11: *The Discipline of Meditation*

THINK ABOUT THIS
Philippians 4:8

Whatever is true...think about such things.

My husband, who is both a seminary professor and a pastor, often has conversations with people who say they are atheists. One of the questions he typically asks an atheist is, "How important is the question of whether God really exists?" Frequently, they respond that they consider the question very important.

He then gently probes deeper and asks, "Since you feel it is important, how is your investigation going? What resources are you reading? To whom are you listening about this important question?" It would be a lop-sided investigation indeed if the only resources one relied upon fell on one side of the issue, and if only antagonistic commentators were consulted.

Do you love God with your mind? Are you aware of the vast well of resources in theology, biblical studies, archaeology, philosophy, and history that undergird our beliefs? Can you show others?

Write below some common objections to faith or questions you might have. Begin reading Christian writers in apologetics (the defense of the faith) such as William Lane Craig, Paul Copan, and C.S. Lewis and dwell on the truth of the gospel.

PRAYER
Heavenly Father, lead me to reliable, truthful resources. Give me a hunger for Your Word and let it nourish my mind. Amen.

_____

_____

_____

_____

_____

_____

UNDERTAKING HOLY DISCIPLINES
Week 12: *The Discipline of the Sabbath*

HOMESICK
Exodus 20:8

Remember the Sabbath day by keeping it holy.

In a letter to his friend Arthur Greeves, C. S. Lewis penned about his anticipation of going home to Ireland: "These last few days! Every little nuisance, every stale or tiresome bit of work, every feeling of that estrangement which I never quite get over in another country, serves as a delightful reminder of how different it will all be soon. Already one's mind dwells upon the sights and sounds and smells of home."

Though Lewis wrote these words years before he came to faith in Christ, they ring with what Lewis called the longing for Joy, that yearning for *Something More* that gradually drew him to Christ. Lewis left his atheism behind as he came to realize that the ache in his heart was a longing for God Himself. The human heart longs for its Maker; it longs for Home.

Sabbath rest, when we come into His presence and worship, should excite our longing for Home. Do you feel that yearning when you worship? Would it be different if you approached worship with a deeper sense of holiness? Reflect on this below.

PRAYER
Heavenly Father, help me to come into your presence with a sense of awe. Convict me of my sin. Amen.

UNDERTAKING HOLY DISCIPLINES
Week 12: *The Discipline of the Sabbath*
MOVING AT THE SPEED OF CHURCH Exodus 20:9-10a

Six days you shall labor and do all your work, but the seventh day is a sabbath to the LORD your God.

Between work, three children, my husband's teaching career, his interim pastor position, and my own responsibilities at church, my schedule was full. Then the letter came. Church members, I was reminded, had agreed to be involved in three components of church life: teaching, serving, and connecting. The letter indicated that I would now be involved in two of the three.

I stared at the letter. The leadership meant well, but I was stunned. I wondered how I could take on more and do any of it well. I wondered what made them think I wasn't doing "enough."

Growing God's kingdom is our number one priority as a community of believers, but making disciples will never happen if we sacrifice rest and personal time with Him.

Is your life running at society's breakneck speed? Do you stop only to catch your breath or to enjoy God's presence? List below your weekly activities and how much time you spend in each. How does it compare to the time you rest in Him?

PRAYER
Heavenly Father, help me resist the cultural pressure to fill every minute of time. Call me to fellowship and rest in You. Amen.

UNDERTAKING HOLY DISCIPLINES
Week 12: *The Discipline of the Sabbath*
LUXURIOUS REST — Exodus 20:10a

But the seventh day is a sabbath to the LORD your God.

I once heard a senior adult marvel at the price and variety of athletic shoes. To an individual who never owned more than one pair of shoes at a time as a child, the specialization of shoes for recreation was overwhelming: one kind for walking, a different kind for running, another for basketball, tennis, biking, and so on.

While the Fourth Commandment makes it clear that humans must have time for rest and relaxation, it was never intended to mean vacation from God. Deep, satisfying rest is only possible in His presence.

In *The Unknown God*, renowned theologian and author Alister McGrath wrote that we fill our lives in vain with everything around us, hoping to find satisfaction and peace: "In the end, only God can satisfy—precisely because we are made to relate to God, and luxuriate in [H]is presence" (p. 120).

Use the space below to describe what it feels like to completely unwind. Does worship on Sunday morning feel like that? What about your time alone with God? Why or why not?

PRAYER
Heavenly Father, remind me that all of my possessions, my achievements, and my work will not truly satisfy. Tune my heart to resonate to Yours. Amen.

UNDERTAKING HOLY DISCIPLINES
Week 12: *The Discipline of the Sabbath*

CHURNING NOISE
Exodus 20:11

For in six days the LORD made the heavens and the earth, the sea, and all that is in them, but he rested on the seventh day. Therefore the LORD blessed the Sabbath day and made it holy.

In an online opinion page of the *New York Times*, Tim Kreider told about contacting a friend to see if they could get together. The friend responded that he was busy, but if "something was going on" to let him know. Kreider wrote back that there would be no forthcoming invitation; that contact was his invitation. "His busyness was like some vast churning noise through which he was shouting out at me, and I gave up trying to shout back over it," Kreider wrote ("The 'Busy' Trap," June 30, 2012).

God ordained Sabbath rest for our own good. We run from one commitment to another, often sprinting past those we love the most. Children give up trying to shout over the noise to their parents; parents wonder what caused the gaping hole between them and their children.

Is your life a "vast churning noise?" List your regular activities below. As you commit each to God, ask Him what He would have you change or rearrange.

PRAYER
Heavenly Father, reveal sins in my life that are fruits of worldliness. Give me a passion for your Word that I may know how to please You. Amen.

MAKING HOLY DISCIPLINES
2: *The Discipline of the Sabbath*

WILL IT BE YOU? Exodus 20:11

Therefore the LORD blessed the Sabbath day and made it holy.

The film *Chariots of Fire* caught the imagination of millions as it told the story of Eric Liddell, the son of missionaries to China who became a 1924 Olympian champion. Liddell withdrew from the 100-meter race, his best event, because it was scheduled on a Sunday. His conviction not to compete on the Sabbath caused him to shift to the 400-meter event, a race at which he had not previously excelled.

Just before the gun sounded for the 400-meter event at the Paris Olympics, Liddell was handed a slip of paper with the words of 1 Samuel 2:30: "Those who honor me I will honor." Liddell won the Gold medal in the 400-meter and broke the existing Olympic and World Records.

Where are the Eric Liddells of today? Will it be you? What impact would it make where you work and live if your life demonstrated to others that following Jesus meant more to you than any honor, friendship, or possession? Record your thoughts below.

PRAYER
Heavenly Father, reveal to me any area of my life that doesn't honor You. Give me the courage and the wisdom to live in a way that does. Amen

USING GOD'S GIFTS WISELY
Week 13: *Gifted With Time*

A NEW LIFE
Ephesians 5:8-10a

For you were once darkness, but now you are light in the Lord. Live as children of light (for the fruit of the light consists in all goodness, righteousness and truth) and find out what pleases the Lord.

Paul began Ephesians 5 with an exhortation to his readers to imitate Christ. Paul then described what a disciple of Christ looked like as he or she daily pursued a life of righteousness. It wasn't that he wanted followers of Christ to simply display moral behavior. On the contrary, he clearly communicated that disciples are not ethically changed human beings—they are new people altogether.

Those who follow Christ once lived with a heart that pursued the things of this world instead of seeking to glorify God. But, those who have truly repented and believed in Christ are new creations. They are not to live as they did before because they are not who they used to be. They do not live for themselves but are representatives of Christ. And this new life for Christ is made evident by a life that pleases the Lord.

Whether your story of faith in Christ is one that is preceded by a lifestyle of being "good" or one that comes after a lifetime of destructive decisions, your life before Christ was one of sinful rebellion, incapable of pleasing God. But you are no longer that person! Hallelujah! Spend a moment thinking about how Christ has changed your life. How are you different because of His redemption? Respond below.

PRAYER
Heavenly Father, thank You for making me new. Help me to leave behind the lifestyle of sinfulness and pursue You and Your righteousness. Amen.

USING GOD'S GIFTS WISELY
Week 13: *Gifted With Time*
DISCERNING WISDOM Ephesians 5:10b–11a

And find out what pleases the Lord. Have nothing to do with the fruitless deeds of darkness, but rather expose them.

In the preceding verses, Paul had described several behaviors that were characteristic of worldly pursuits—the fruits of sinfulness and darkness. Sins such as sexual immorality and idolatry were evidence of a life lived in opposition to God and were not to be associated with one who followed Christ. A disciple was to run from these sins.

Paul noted that a disciple is not only to be known by his or her abstention from sin but because a disciple exposes sin in the pursuit of pleasing the Lord. The Bible gives many principles for righteous living, and these principles must be the scale by which a disciple weighs decisions and actions. The world is full of many specific circumstances which the Bible does not acutely address. Paul, however, noted that Scripture is not irrelevant in any situation. In partnership with the Holy Spirit, the disciple must seek wisdom from God to discern how to please Him in all of life's challenges. This is a disciple's motivation—to please the Lord by living according to His Word.

Think for a moment about what your primary motivation is—pleasing the Lord? Pleasing others? Pleasing your family? How does this motivation affect the way that you make decisions? What does it reflect about who is in charge of your life?

PRAYER
Heavenly Father, reveal sins in my life that are fruits of worldliness. Give me a passion for your Word that I may know how to please You. Amen.

USING GOD'S GIFTS WISELY
Week 13: *Gifted With Time*

EXPOSING SIN
Ephesians 5:11b–14

Have nothing to do with the fruitless deeds of darkness, but rather expose them. It is shameful even to mention what the disobedient do in secret. But everything exposed by the light becomes visible—and everything that is illuminated becomes a light. This is why it is said: "Wake up, sleeper, rise from the dead, and Christ will shine on you."

Paul admonished his readers to live as followers of Christ who purposefully sought to please the Lord. He continued that thought with contrasting imagery: the righteousness of the light with the sinfulness of the dark. This juxtaposition of simple and familiar notions—that of light and dark—clearly give a picture of the disciple's new life in the light of Christ instead of his former abode in darkness.

Using the word "expose," Paul noted that living in the light meant an active attack against sin. A disciple is to continually uncover the existence of sin in his or her own life as well as in the greater community of God's people. To live a life pleasing to God, the disciple must ask God to seek out the sin in his or her life and then ask Him to destroy it. To follow Christ in full obedience is to pursue a life of holiness, as He is holy. Therefore, the new life of a Christian is to be one that desires to purge all sin. As Paul pointed out, sin is exposed when the Light of Christ shines on it. And His light will bring life to the one who had been dead in sin.

Do you have "guilty pleasure" sins that you consider harmless? What does a lighthearted approach to sin indicate about one's relationship with Christ? What can you practically do to begin exposing the sin in your life?

PRAYER
Heavenly Father, convict me of sin in my life, and give me victory over it. May I never regard sin flippantly but, instead, pursue a life of holiness through Your power. Amen.

USING GOD'S GIFTS WISELY
Week 13: *Gifted With Time*
REDEEMING THE TIME   Ephesians 5:15-16

Be very careful, then, how you live—not as unwise but as wise, making the most of every opportunity, because the days are evil.

In light of the serious nature of sin and the disciple's call to live in the light of Christ's righteousness, Paul warned his readers to be careful about how they spent their time. As one who is to spend his life in obedience to the Lord and in response to His command to make disciples, a Christ follower must view his life as belonging to God.

Christ did not redeem His followers simply for their own happiness. No, He gave them new life and called them to be His representatives. This truth not only means that a disciple is to discern how to live according to the Word of God but also that she entirely belongs to Him. Time is a precious commodity because its moments make up an entire lifetime and cannot be repeated. Paul wanted his readers to be aware that they were surrounded by evil. Instead of hiding from their surroundings, however, Paul encouraged them to seek God's wisdom in knowing how to live a holy life—minute by minute—so that their lives were not wasted.

Take a moment and look at your calendar. How does it reflect someone who seeks to make every moment glorify God? How much time do you waste in disobedience to God? What kind of attitude shift do you need to make concerning the purpose and ownership of your time? Respond below.

PRAYER
Heavenly Father, show me where I am disobedient to You in my time. Forgive me for how I have been selfish and possessive of my time instead of recognizing that it belongs fully to You. Amen.

_____

_____

_____

_____

_____

USING GOD'S GIFTS WISELY
Week 13: *Gifted With Time*

MAKING IT COUNT
Ephesians 5:16b–17

Making the most of every opportunity, because the days are evil. Therefore do not be foolish, but understand what the Lord's will is.

A recurring theme in this week's verses has been the idea of discerning the will of God. Paul did not intend for his readers to think that they had to try to understand everything about God. Scripture is clear that He has revealed Himself sufficiently through His Word, and that His followers must use this revelation (the Bible) as guidelines for their lives.

Paul knew that living in a world full of evil brings many temptations to followers of Christ. These temptations could be simple distractions or deep sin. Either way, a disciple who has been influenced apart from God is one who is wasting opportunities. To be aware of these temptations and opportunities, a disciple must be a student of God's revelation. In addition, a disciple never knows how many days he has left upon this earth, but all of them belong to God. To spend them on foolishness is to waste them. Therefore, a disciple makes his life count by living according to God's Word and His will.

Think about how you make decisions. How do you seek to know God's will and apply it to every decision you make? What do you want your life to count for? Respond below.

PRAYER
Heavenly Father, thank You for giving us Your Word so that we could know You and Your will. Please develop a love for Your Word in my heart so that I can live purposefully for You. Amen.

_____

_____

_____

_____

_____

USING GOD'S GIFTS WISELY
Week 14: *Gifted With Skills*

PROVIDER
Exodus 31:1–6

Then the LORD said to Moses, "See, I have chosen Bezalel son of Uri, the son of Hur, of the tribe of Judah, and I have filled him with the Spirit of God, with wisdom, with understanding, with knowledge and with all kinds of skills—to make artistic designs for work in gold, silver and bronze, to cut and set stones, to work in wood, and to engage in all kinds of crafts. Moreover, I have appointed Oholiab son of Ahisamak, of the tribe of Dan, to help him. Also I have given ability to all the skilled workers to make everything I have commanded you.

God came to Moses—a fugitive living in the desert—and called him to lead the Israelites out of slavery in Egypt. Through miraculous wonders, God did all that He promised Moses, and the Israelites found themselves on a journey to the Promise Land, again fulfilling His word. Through the leadership of Moses, God entered into covenant with them through His Law. In His Law, God gave instructions to build a place of worship—the place where His presence would dwell with them.

God had proven Himself faithful, and His Tabernacle would remind the people of that faithfulness. God told Moses that He had gifted men with the skills needed to completely fulfill every detail. God gave Moses an incredible task, but He provided everything that was needed to fulfill it. He had worked this way with Moses' leadership abilities, in bringing the Israelites out of slavery, and in the tiniest of details for the Tabernacle. God did not give commands without providing. Disciples can and must faithfully obey God when He instructs because He is faithful to fulfill His promises and to provide everything we need to obey.

How have you seen God provide in your life? Have you ever hesitated to obey Him out of fear of provision? Take a moment and write down a list of how God has proven Himself faithful to you.

PRAYER
Heavenly Father, I praise You for Your great faithfulness and Your desire to provide for Your children. Give me strength to obey You in light of Your faithful character. Amen.

USING GOD'S GIFTS WISELY
Week 14: *Gifted With Skills*

CALLED AND EQUIPPED Exodus 31:2–5

See, I have chosen Bezalel son of Uri, the son of Hur, of the tribe of Judah, and I have filled him with the Spirit of God, with wisdom, with understanding, with knowledge and with all kinds of skills—to make artistic designs for work in gold, silver and bronze, to cut and set stones, to work in wood, and to engage in all kinds of crafts

God made a list for Moses of all of the skills that Bezalel possessed and how they would be helpful in building the Tabernacle. These skills, however, were not simply natural talents that Bezalel had developed over the years. God clearly noted that it was His Spirit that had gifted this man for the work that he would do for the Lord.

God sovereignly knew the monumental task that was before the Israelites, and He gifted Bezalel for such a task. The artistic creativity, wisdom, ability, and knowledge were gifts of God, not human accomplishment. Bezalel likely put forth effort in honing and developing these skills over his lifetime, but it was God's ultimate plan that directed Bezalel so that he was ready for the calling that God gave him. God called him, and God equipped him. Therefore, all of Bezalel's abilities were for the glory of God alone. A disciple is called to serve God with every skill and talent because they are all from God and for His glory.

Consider the following questions and respond below. What natural skills and abilities do you have? Do you view them as personal accomplishments or gifts from God? How are you being faithful to develop these skills so that when opportunities and callings arise, you can be obedient to God's calling and use your skills for His glory?

PRAYER
Heavenly Father, forgive me for the ways that I have been lazy or misused my giftedness. Help me to be faithful to develop my skills now so that I will be ready for opportunities that You bring me. Amen.

USING GOD'S GIFTS WISELY
Week 14: *Gifted With Skills*
SERVICE GIFTS
Exodus 31:6

Moreover, I have appointed Oholiab son of Ahisamak, of the tribe of Dan, to help him. Also I have given ability to all the skilled workers to make everything I have commanded you.

Bezalel was not the only skilled worker that God had called. Oholiab and other unnamed craftsmen were also key to the completion of the Tabernacle. All of their various gifts came together under the sovereignty of God for His purposes—for His ministry.

These men were not priests; they were craftsmen. And yet they were essential pieces of God's will and plan for His people. They may not have thought of themselves as having much to offer in the spiritual worship of God, but their skills were gifts of God to be used to bring glory to His name. All disciples are called by God for His service, no matter what their skills or their occupation. God has specifically gifted and called each of His people to be faithful where He has placed them and with the tools with which He has equipped them. They work daily for His glory in their sphere of influence.

Have you ever felt inadequate to make a difference for God because your skills aren't often seen as beneficial to the kingdom of God? Why is this attitude not reflective of God's call? Think for a moment about the skills that you have and how they place you in a unique sphere of influence. How can you use your skills and position to glorify God and to make disciples?

PRAYER
Heavenly Father, thank You for gifting me and allowing me to use those gifts for Your glory. Empower me to boldly use the skills You've given me to impact the world for You. Amen.

USING GOD'S GIFTS WISELY
Week 14: *Gifted With Skills*

SERVICE GIFTS

Exodus 31:6–11

Moreover, I have appointed Oholiab son of Ahisamak, of the tribe of Dan, to help him. Also I have given ability to all the skilled workers to make everything I have commanded you: the tent of meeting, the ark of the covenant law with the atonement cover on it, and all the other furnishings of the tent—the table and its articles, the pure gold lampstand and all its accessories, the altar of incense, the altar of burnt offering and all its utensils, the basin with its stand—and also the woven garments, both the sacred garments for Aaron the priest and the garments for his sons when they serve as priests, and the anointing oil and fragrant incense for the Holy Place. They are to make them just as I commanded you

God's instructions for the Tabernacle included much work and many people to complete it. God gifted all of these craftsmen so that each task could be completed well. This project was too great for one man to accomplish. Rather, numerous people were required to lead, guide, and work to complete it.

Bezalel stood out as a craftsman who was multi-talented. God abundantly gifted Bezalel to do much of the work needed on the Tabernacle. Still, God did not expect him to work alone. No, numerous craftsmen were gifted and called. Some may have had one specialty while others were Renaissance men like Bezalel. But the truth remains that God gifted them to work together for His purposes. Disciples have various skills, and all of them are important in the work of God. He did not create His people to live in isolation; nor did He create them to work alone. The gifts God has given His people are to be used in community—to accomplish His work and bring glory to Him.

Think creatively about how you can use your skills within the Body of Christ. Are there existing ministries in your area that could use a person with your skill set? How can your skills contribute to the work of the kingdom?

PRAYER
Heavenly Father, forgive me for trying to work for You alone. Open my eyes to see opportunities to work in community for Your glory. Amen.

USING GOD'S GIFTS WISELY
Week 14: *Gifted With Skills*

IN THE DETAILS — Exodus 31:1–11

Then the Lord said to Moses, "See, I have chosen Bezalel son of Uri, the son of Hur, of the tribe of Judah, and I have filled him with the Spirit of God, with wisdom, with understanding, with knowledge and with all kinds of skills—to make artistic designs for work in gold, silver and bronze, to cut and set stones, to work in wood, and to engage in all kinds of crafts. Moreover, I have appointed Oholiab son of Ahisamak, of the tribe of Dan, to help him. Also I have given ability to all the skilled workers to make everything I have commanded you: the tent of meeting, the ark of the covenant law with the atonement cover on it, and all the other furnishings of the tent—the table and its articles, the pure gold lampstand and all its accessories, the altar of incense, the altar of burnt offering and all its utensils, the basin with its stand—and also the woven garments, both the sacred garments for Aaron the priest and the garments for his sons when they serve as priests, and the anointing oil and fragrant incense for the Holy Place. They are to make them just as I commanded you."

The sheer list of details regarding the building of the Tabernacle reveals a great characteristic of the God who gave those instructions: He is the God of details as well as the One who provides the means and skills to fulfill His instructions. Neither Moses nor the craftsmen had to guess how God wanted His Tabernacle built. The instructions were clear and complete, and His provision was more than sufficient.

Moses did not need to worry about God forgetting or overlooking a single detail. All of His words and all of His provision were more than adequate to fulfill the task. The details of a disciple's calling can be overwhelming. And leading out into the unknown is unnerving if one does not believe that God is involved in the details as much as the big picture. All that God provides—in information and provision—is sufficient for His disciples to live in full obedience to Him, no matter how incomplete they seem at the time. God's people can rest in the assurance that the God who created them is sovereign over the tiniest detail.

How does faith in God's sovereignty over the details give freedom to obey fully? How does this truth lead you to trust in God in all circumstances? Respond below.

PRAYER
Heavenly Father, forgive me for becoming anxious over details of my life even though I know You are sovereign over them. Help me to balance my responsibility to act with my faith that You are in control. Amen.

USING GOD'S GIFTS WISELY
Week 15: *Gifted With Contentment*
TO KNOW HIM
1 Timothy 6:5

And constant friction between people of corrupt mind, who have been robbed of the truth and who think that godliness is a means to financial gain.

Paul warned Timothy often about false teachers, and such is the immediate context for this verse. Paul stated that anything which contradicts the truth of Christ's teachings is a false gospel. Paul wrote that false teachers disregard the truth and cause destruction among the Body of Christ. Falling under this heading of false teachers were those who preached that godliness would bring financial gain as a result of God's favor.

That Paul called this belief a false teaching is telling of the level of harm that it can bring to the lives of believers. Looking at the lives of Jesus' disciples in the New Testament, followers of Christ know that this teaching is not true. Even His disciples experienced great trials and death as a result of their unrelenting commitment to follow Christ in faith. Godliness is not a means to wealthy prosperity. To believe otherwise is to create a life that pursues God for selfish benefits rather than to pursue God for the sake of knowing God. A disciple's life is not his own; therefore, his motivation cannot be for his own gain but for the sake of knowing Christ and the power of His true gospel.

How has your motivation for following Christ been influenced by selfish desires? Why is knowing God infinitely greater than personal prosperity?

PRAYER
Heavenly Father, if there is any sin in my heart toward following You, convict me. Create in me a heart that strives to know You above everything else. Make knowing You my life's ambition. Amen.

USING GOD'S GIFTS WISELY
Week 15: *Gifted With Contentment*
ETERNAL PERSPECTIVE   1 Timothy 6:6-7

But godliness with contentment is great gain. For we brought nothing into the world, and we can take nothing out of it.

After identifying a false gospel that relates godliness with financial prosperity, Paul then contrasted financial gain with the great gain that one finds with contentment. He asserted that godliness with contentment is what brings peace and focus in this life. And, how does a disciple gain such contentment in the midst of a world that strives for financial prosperity? Paul told Timothy that the answer is maintaining an eternal perspective.

Paul bluntly reminded Timothy that this world is temporary. Those who live in this world didn't bring anything with them, and they will leave the same way. Therefore, Christians must remember that only that which is eternal will last, and accumulated wealth is not part of that list. Disciples live in a distracted world, with numerous pursuits vying for their attention. But when they remember that this world is not their eternal home, priorities shift and foolish pursuits are loosened to blow away in the wind. When a disciple can continually maintain an eternal perspective, he or she will be able to discern what matters and what is worth their time, money, and energy.

If you examined your daily and weekly priorities, what would they reveal about your focus on eternal matters? If you could leave a legacy for generations after you, what would you want it to be? Respond below.

PRAYER
Heavenly Father, show me the ways I am wasting my life by investing in things that won't last. Help me to focus on You and realize that all of Your blessings in my life are to be used for Your glory in the world. Amen.

USING GOD'S GIFTS WISELY
Week 15: *Gifted With Contentment*
SUFFICIENTLY CONTENT   1 Timothy 6:8

But if we have food and clothing, we will be content with that.

Paul explained to Timothy that having an eternal perspective is essential for contentment. He then defined contentment as being in a position of living sufficiently—having just enough—as he contrasted riches with the minimum for physical survival. Paul argued that when a disciple is consumed with doing God's will, he or she is not bullied by the desire for more but lives joyfully and happily with the simplicity of sufficiency.

Paul did not want Timothy to disregard caring for the physical needs of others or to abandon his responsibility to provide for those in his care. In truth, Paul benefitted from the generosity of others who were able to support him. Yet their attitude toward their resources was what enabled them to use their finances for God's work instead of accumulating more and more wealth. When a disciple is content with God's provision for his or her life, he is able to maintain an attitude of sufficiency, which pushes him to give more as he is able and to disregard materialism because he is content with that which lasts eternally.

Considering your surrounding culture, why is contentment difficult to maintain? How do you balance the call to live with sufficient guidelines without being legalistic? What is the difference between living in sufficiency and living for more? Respond below.

PRAYER
Heavenly Father, draw my heart to You that I may know that You are all that I need. Thank You for Your provision, and forgive me for the times that I am ungrateful for what You've given me. Amen.

USING GOD'S GIFTS WISELY
Week 15: *Gifted With Contentment*

IDOL WORSHIP
1 Timothy 6:9–10

Those who want to get rich fall into temptation and a trap and into many foolish and harmful desires that plunge people into ruin and destruction. For the love of money is a root of all kinds of evil. Some people, eager for money, have wandered from the faith and pierced themselves with many griefs.

Paul continued to warn Timothy about the problems that pursuing wealth could bring. He did not shy away from boldly claiming that those people who are motivated by the pursuit of becoming rich are foolishly following a dangerous path. Paul did not hate money. He recognized its necessity in life. In fact, he did not teach that money was evil; rather, he taught that loving money was the root of much sin.

Paul taught that loving money is an indicator that wealth has become an idol—it has taken the place of God. Paul called this idol a trap because, he argued, it leads people to worship money and the pursuit of it; yet, only God has the rightful place of being worshiped. Idols not only steal God's glory, they also enslave. Someone who is consumed with collecting wealth is enslaved by an insatiable desire for more—more things that cannot bring satisfaction. Disciples must examine if materialism has taken over God's rightful place in their heart. Although money is not inherently evil, disciples must be careful to not let it become a motivator in their lives.

How freely do you hold onto your money? Are you willing to use it for God's glory or do you hoard it for personal luxuries? How can you tell if money drives the decisions you make in life?

PRAYER
Heavenly Father, I confess that money can become the object of my heart, and I am not content with what I have. Help me to be a good steward of what You have given me so I can use it for Your glory around the world. Amen.

USING GOD'S GIFTS WISELY
Week 15: *Gifted With Contentment*
HOLY PURSUIT 1 Timothy 6:11

But you, man of God, flee from all this, and pursue righteousness, godliness, faith, love, endurance and gentleness.

Paul used the phrase man of God to contrast Timothy with the false teachers from previous verses. Timothy preached the true gospel, and he followed God for the sake of knowing Him and not for financial gain.

Paul instructed Timothy to beware of those who teach that the gospel brings financial gain in this world. In contrast to their pursuit of the idol of wealth, Timothy was to pursue the truth of righteous living. He was to run away from the false doctrine as quickly as he could and run toward godliness. Disciples are not to be known solely by what they run from; they must also be known by who they are and the way their lives are characterized by the attributes of God. When a disciple pursues God instead of the things God can do for him, he becomes more like Christ. And when a disciple exhibits Christ in her life, others see the true gospel lived out among them—one that centers around who God is and not how He can benefit His people materially.

If others had to describe you using three words, which ones would they use? Does this description look more like God or the world you live in? How does the pursuit of godliness lead you to contentment instead of materialism?

PRAYER
Heavenly Father, draw my heart near to You. Give me a passion for You and Your word that I may know You and reflect You in my life. Amen.

_____

_____

_____

_____

USING GOD'S GIFTS WISELY
Week 16: *Gifted for Him*
STEWARDS FOR ANOTHER — Matthew 25:14–15

Again, it will be like a man going on a journey, who called his servants and entrusted his wealth to them. To one he gave five bags of gold, to another two bags, and to another one bag, each according to his ability. Then he went on his journey.

Jesus often taught in parables, and this teaching story is one of three that He used to warn His followers that they should be ready for His return. In this parable, being ready for Him meant that Jesus' followers recognized their stewardship of His resources and faithfully used them for His glory.

The man going on a journey represents Christ, and the servants represent His disciples. Jesus used the concrete example of money as a representative of all resources that His followers have—from skills and giftedness to more tangible resources such as wealth. Jesus clearly indicated that the one who called his servants was the one to whom the resources belonged. The servants were entrusted with what already belonged to their master; it was not their own and neither was it the result of their investments. Followers of Jesus are His stewards because nothing they have belongs to them. Rather, all of their resources have been entrusted to their care on behalf of Him. Therefore, their responsibility is to faithfully use their resources for His glory. He does not give gifts for the sake of a disciple's happiness but for the proclamation of His glory in the earth.

Think about what resources you have available—money, time, energy, skills, material items. Below, record how you can specifically use these resources for the glory of God.

PRAYER
Heavenly Father, forgive me for the many times that I do not acknowledge that all that I have is Yours. Open my eyes to see opportunities to faithfully use my resources for Your glory. Amen.

_____

_____

_____

USING GOD'S GIFTS WISELY
Week 16: *Gifted for Him*

FAITHFUL USE Matthew 25:15–18

To one he gave five bags of gold, to another two bags, and to another one bag, each according to his ability. Then he went on his journey. The man who had received five bags of gold went at once and put his money to work and gained five bags more. So also, the one with two bags of gold gained two more. But the man who had received one bag went off, dug a hole in the ground and hid his master's money.

In this parable, the master gave his servants different amounts of money, each according to the master's discretion. The servants had varying resources, but their responsibility was the same—to be good stewards of what the master had entrusted to them. The master was not showing favoritism to one servant and punishing another by giving different amounts of money. It was simply up to the master's wisdom to give his grace as he saw best.

Jesus did not hide the fact that God blesses His people with different resources or abilities. They are all gifts of grace and are not evidence of God playing favorites. It's easy to look around the Body of Christ and compare ourselves with others, but it is not a disciple's place to question God's wisdom. Rather, she is to be faithful in what she has been given. All gifts are God's gifts for the sake of His Body—not for the benefit of its members. The point of the parable wasn't the different gifts but what the servants did with them. Likewise, disciples aren't to compare gifts but to be faithful to use them for God's glory.

What skills or gifts do you think are "better" than what you have? Why? Why is comparing with other believers detrimental to the unity of the Body of Christ?

PRAYER
Heavenly Father, thank You for the grace You have shown me in allowing me to be a steward of Your resources. Show me how to confidently use the gifts You've given for Your glory. Amen.

USING GOD'S GIFTS WISELY
Week 16: *Gifted for Him*
FAITHFUL SERVANTS — Matthew 25:19-23

"After a long time the master of those servants returned and settled accounts with them. The man who had received five bags of gold brought the other five. 'Master,' he said, 'you entrusted me with five bags of gold. See, I have gained five more.' "His master replied, 'Well done, good and faithful servant! You have been faithful with a few things; I will put you in charge of many things. Come and share your master's happiness!' "The man with two bags of gold also came. 'Master,' he said, 'you entrusted me with two bags of gold; see, I have gained two more.' "His master replied, 'Well done, good and faithful servant! You have been faithful with a few things; I will put you in charge of many things. Come and share your master's happiness!'"

The master in this parable praised the two servants who displayed faithful stewardship on his behalf. They carefully and intelligently sought to invest what he had given them. Their faithful use of their resources allowed these servants to demonstrate not only their desire to please the one they served but that they gladly honored him with their actions concerning the gifts he entrusted to them.

When telling this story, Jesus used the same exact phrase when addressing the master's praise for the two faithful servants. This identical usage communicated that the master was overjoyed for both servants, regardless of the size of their return on investment. God gives gifts to His disciples in varying sizes and degrees—resources that will produce an outcome of varying sizes and degrees. The important point is not the outcome but that the disciple is faithful in using his resources as a steward of God's gifts. Faithfulness in stewardship reveals a desire to please God and a joy in honoring Him. Therefore, the condition of a disciple's heart toward God is revealed in his stewardship.

Why do we tend to focus on those gifts that draw lots of attention and neglect those that are necessary but less "glorious" than others? What resources are you ignoring because of apathy? How can you help others to use their resources and gifts faithfully?

PRAYER
Heavenly Father, show me any ways that I am not faithful in my stewardship of Your gifts. Draw me to You that I may serve You with a joyful heart. Amen.

USING GOD'S GIFTS WISELY
Week 16: *Gifted for Him*
EXCUSES
Matthew 25:24–28

"Then the man who had received one bag of gold came. 'Master,' he said, 'I knew that you are a hard man, harvesting where you have not sown and gathering where you have not scattered seed. So I was afraid and went out and hid your gold in the ground. See, here is what belongs to you.' His master replied, 'You wicked, lazy servant! So you knew that I harvest where I have not sown and gather where I have not scattered seed? Well then, you should have put my money on deposit with the bankers, so that when I returned I would have received it back with interest. So take the bag of gold from him and give it to the one who has ten bags.'"

After praising two servants who were eager to please the master, one servant remained, who approached the master with misguided fear. Not only did this servant display a sordid attitude toward stewardship, he questioned the very character of the master. The servant explained away his apathy by falsely claiming that the master was difficult, manipulative, and unethical.

Jesus gave no indication as to why the servant made these claims, but He revealed that they were false. Either the servant simply was lazy and used fear as an excuse for inaction or he truly (and falsely) believed that his master was unkind and greedy—or possibly both. Despite his excuses, his lack of knowledge and relationship with his master was obvious, as he knew neither the desires of his master nor the character of his master. In truth, his excuse for stewardship was a result of his lack of relationship. Discipleship happens in the course of relationship with Christ. A believer who does not spend time getting to know Christ will inevitably question His character and His commands. A disciple, however, knows who her master is and desires to please Him with everything she has.

What are some of your excuses for not obeying God? Do you know how to obey God fully as a result of knowing His character as He has revealed it in Scripture?

PRAYER
Heavenly Father, thank You for the grace You have shown me in allowing me to be a steward of Your resources. Show me how to confidently use the gifts You've given for Your glory. Amen.

USING GOD'S GIFTS WISELY
Week 16: *Gifted for Him*
GIVEN MORE   Matthew 25:29-30

"For whoever has will be given more, and they will have an abundance. Whoever does not have, even what they have will be taken from them. And throw that worthless servant outside, into the darkness, where there will be weeping and gnashing of teeth."

The master expected obedience and complete loyalty, and he rewarded it with more opportunities for service. As for the lazy servant, his lack of relationship with the master was revealed, and he was thrown out. He never knew the master and did not care to please him by meeting his expectations.

The master had expectations, and those that knew him were excited to do everything they could to meet them and honor him with their success. They used their resources wisely, and the master rewarded them with more—not just more resources but more opportunities to serve him faithfully. When disciples are faithful to use their resources for the glory of God and seek to please Him in all that they do, God rewards their faithfulness with even more opportunities. Disciples should take note that God does not always give more resources: the master in the parable only gave more resources to one servant, although he praised both for their work. He does, however, open avenues for disciples to have additional opportunities to honor Him with their stewardship.

Consider your motivations to obey God. Do they reveal a vibrant relationship with Him or one that does not exist? How is God opening more opportunities for you to serve Him by glorifying Him with your resources?

PRAYER
Heavenly Father, open my eyes to see when You are opening new doors of service for me. Guide me in knowing when You are working and when I am forcing new opportunities to happen. Amen.

USING GOD'S GIFTS WISELY
Week 17: *Gifted for the Body*
EQUAL GRACE
Romans 12:3

For by the grace given me I say to every one of you: Do not think of yourself more highly than you ought, but rather think of yourself with sober judgment, in accordance with the faith God has distributed to each of you.

Paul had dealt with the tendency of believers within church bodies to prioritize the gifts of the Spirit, valuing some gifts such as prophecy or teaching over others. When addressing the issue of spiritual gifts to the church at Rome, Paul wanted them to understand the imperative nature of the unity of their gifts. In doing so, they would recognize that all spiritual gifts are gifts of grace and are not for inflating anyone's ego.

Paul admonished the believers at Rome to think of themselves with "sober judgment" instead of haughty attitudes. The truth of their giftedness was not in and of themselves but in the grace of God to bestow any gifts at all. They did nothing to earn God's favor, His grace, or His gifts. Therefore, they had nothing to boast about except the work of God in their lives. Likewise, there is no place for self-aggrandizing in the Body of Christ. A disciple is to view all of his gifts in view of God's mercy. In doing so, he can only see his identity as founded on Christ and nothing he could possibly have done himself—removing any temptation for a big ego.

Consider the ways that you (possibly secretly) compare yourself to others. What does that reveal about your attitude toward giftedness and the grace of God at work in your life?

PRAYER
Heavenly Father, there are many ways that I have an inflated view of myself. Forgive me for thinking so little of Your grace that I neglect to acknowledge Your work in my life. Amen.

TOGETHER
Romans 12:4-5

For just as each of us has one body with many members, and these members do not all have the same function, so in Christ we, though many, form one body, and each member belongs to all the others.

In light of the fact that the gifts of the Spirit were gracious gifts of God, Paul continued to encourage the church at Rome to not only relinquish any egotistical thoughts but also to recognize that each member of the body was essential for God's work.

Because these spiritual gifts were given by God, Paul rightly concluded that God was intentional in how they were distributed. God was not mindless when He bestowed His gifts of grace. The God of details uniquely equipped each of His followers so that they could work together with other believers for His glory. That Paul referred to the Church as a body is not by accident. This imagery gives a concrete example of how disciples are to work together to accomplish God's work in the world. This unity is how God designed His gifts to work. Each disciple is uniquely gifted to contribute to the health and unity of the Body of Christ so that God's mission is accomplished through their collaborative work.

How is your giftedness different from others in your church? How do your unique gifts enable you to contribute to God's mission through the church? Is your involvement in ministry reflective of your belief that God values your gifts?

PRAYER
Heavenly Father, forgive me for the ways I have not contributed to the health of the Body and Your work through it. Reveal Your gifts in my life and show me how to use them in my sphere of influence. Amen.

USING GOD'S GIFTS WISELY
Week 17: *Gifted for the Body*

NOT ALONE
Romans 12:4-5

For just as each of us has one body with many members, and these members do not all have the same function, so in Christ we, though many, form one body, and each member belongs to all the others.

Paul, in identifying believers as essential parts of the Body of Christ, ever so slightly continued the idea by noting that every inch of a body is composed of parts that belong together. At first, this thought seems to be a fairly insignificant way to illustrate this immediate truth; however, upon further consideration, it is quite noteworthy.

When a body is born into the world, each person contains unique DNA, which sets him or her apart from anyone else. Similarly, every disciple has an identifying spiritual component through Christ, which sets him or her apart from the world. As a result, the daily work of God through His disciples can be lonely and will be full of struggles. God never intended for disciples to live in isolation, and Paul boldly calls this truth to attention when he clearly reminded believers that they belong to one another. The implications of this truth are that no one is left behind in the work of God, and no one has the right to attempt to do His work alone. Disciples nurture other disciples and they invite others along in what God is doing around the world.

When are you most tempted to ignore other believers in your attempts at ministry? Why? How are you actively nurturing other believers, specifically less mature ones?

PRAYER
Heavenly Father, forgive me for the excuses I make for attempting to live for You without the help of other believers. Bring people into my life that I may partner with in life and in work for You. Amen.

USING GOD'S GIFTS WISELY
Week 17: Gifted for the Body

CONFIDENT GIFTS — Romans 12:6–8

We have different gifts, according to the grace given to each of us. If your gift is prophesying, then prophesy in accordance with your faith; if it is serving, then serve; if it is teaching, then teach; if it is to encourage, then give encouragement; if it is giving, then give generously; if it is to lead, do it diligently; if it is to show mercy, do it cheerfully.

Paul summed up this passage about spiritual gifts by once again drawing attention to the truth that God has given a variety of gifts to His people for their unified work to accomplish His mission. He asserted that in light of the value of all gifts, believers should confidently use their gifts according to God's grace.

Paul didn't mean that only those with the gift of service should ever serve or that only those with the gift of mercy should ever show mercy. No, all of the spiritual gifts are characteristics that Scripture calls on believers to exhibit. But, disciples are specifically gifted in one or more areas where they can naturally and passionately serve God through the Body. Paul called on the Romans to embrace their gifts and to find a place to use them. Disciples are not to squander their spiritual gifts; God gave these gifts for a purpose. Whether through an inventory or the observations of fellow believers, disciples should identify their gifts and then find a place to use them confidently—because all gifts are gifts of grace and of great value.

Have you identified one or more of your spiritual gifts? If yes, what are they? Where in your local church can you use those gifts to maximize the health of that body? Respond below.

PRAYER
Heavenly Father, thank You for Your gifts of grace in my life. Open my eyes to opportunities to use these in my local church for Your glory. Amen.

USING GOD'S GIFTS WISELY
Week 17: *Gifted for the Body*

WITH THANKFUL HEARTS
Romans 12:6-8

We have different gifts, according to the grace given to each of us. If your gift is prophesying, then prophesy in accordance with your faith; if it is serving, then serve; if it is teaching, then teach; if it is to encourage, then give encouragement; if it is giving, then give generously; if it is to lead, do it diligently; if it is to show mercy, do it cheerfully.

Paul told the believers at Rome to confidently use their spiritual gifts. But he didn't stop there. He instructed them to use their gifts joyfully and with glad hearts. They weren't to go about their lives begrudgingly leading or giving. They were to use their gifts as if they were serving the Lord and not man.

Look at the adverbs Paul used to describe how these believers should use their gifts: *generously, diligently,* and *cheerfully*. Within their specific contexts, these adverbs essentially say, "Use this gift to its fullest. Use it well and go all out." Spiritual gifts are for the glory of God and the edification of the Body of Christ. When not lived out with intentionality and passion in a believer's life, spiritual gifts reflect poorly upon the Giver and the Body. To live with proper thanksgiving to God for His gracious generosity, disciples must display His grace by displaying His gifts as God intended—with full intensity. To do otherwise reveals a heart that is less than thankful. A right action can simply be moral behavior; a right action with a thankful and humble heart is being a disciple who lives in the grace of God.

Think about recent times of ministry in your life. What did your attitude reflect about your heart? How is it possible to change your attitude?

PRAYER
Heavenly Father, I want to serve You with thankfulness and joy, but I can't do it without You. Please work in my heart. Let Your Spirit change me that I may reflect Your grace to others. Amen.

USING GOD'S GIFTS WISELY
Week 18: *Gifted to Love*
CALL FOR PRAYER
1 Peter 4:7

The end of all things is near. Therefore be alert and of sober mind so that you may pray.

Peter also wrote about spiritual gifts. And then he transitioned by calling his readers to prayer. How does prayer fit within the scope of living out one's spiritual gifts? Peter answered that question at end of this passage in verse 11. Verses 7 and 11 provide bookends of the relationship between knowing God and living out His spiritual gifts.

Peter first noted that prayer is essential to live for God's glory. He stated that the time is short. Therefore, believers must seriously consider how they are responsible for the short time that they have on earth. In being stewards of their time, they must maintain their relationship with God. Specifically, Peter noted that communication with God is essential to being ready for Christ's return and for living in a way that honors Him. Prayer is essential because it unites a disciple's heart with God's plan. Prayer guides a disciple as he seeks to know how to best use his gifts for God's mission. To accomplish this purpose, the disciple must spend time listening to God, seeking His face in addition to making requests.

What role does prayer play in your walk with Christ? Do you use it as a time to only make requests of God or is also a time of seeking and listening? Respond below.

PRAYER
Heavenly Father, show me how to spend time in communion with You through prayer. Speak to my heart as I listen to You and seek Your face. Amen.

USING GOD'S GIFTS WISELY
Week 18: *Gifted to Love*
LOVE ABOVE ALL 1 Peter 4:8-9

Above all, love each other deeply, because love covers over a multitude of sins. Offer hospitality to one another without grumbling.

Peter recognized that people are sinful. Although the Holy Spirit lives within each believer, the sinful nature he or she was born with will not be fully eradicated until heaven. In the meantime, Peter acknowledged that the sinful nature would come out, even in the use of spiritual gifts.

Knowing that God demonstrated love first for His people, Peter encouraged his readers to love—an abiding love that selflessly seeks the best for others with no thought of what one could gain in return. It is this kind of love, Peter said, that would cover a multitude of sins. Disciples do not live in isolation, and therefore, there will be conflict. Friendships, marriages, families, and churches—all will experience struggling relationships at times because these relationships are comprised of sinful individuals. Even in seeking how to best use resources and spiritual gifts, a disciple will mess up. She will offer a meal with bitterness. He will lead with manipulation. And yet, love requires confrontation...those who offend must seek forgiveness, and those who are offended must forgive. With love, a disciple provides a safe place for growth and maturity in the journey of becoming more like Christ.

Who in your life needs to be reminded of your love? From whom do you need to seek forgiveness? Respond below, and then take action.

PRAYER
Heavenly Father, forgive me for the times I don't willingly offer love to others. Thank You for loving me when I am not worthy. Amen.

USING GOD'S GIFTS WISELY
Week 18: *Gifted to Love*

HERE TO SERVE — 1 Peter 4:10

Each of you should use whatever gift you have received to serve others, as faithful stewards of God's grace in its various forms.

Peter reminded his readers that they were stewards of God's grace, and using their spiritual gifts was part of their responsibility. As stewards, Christ followers are His representatives; they are caring for or maintaining something that is not theirs for the sake of its rightful owner.

Keeping this truth in mind is essential for a disciple to maintain a rightful attitude toward resources and spiritual gifts. Like salvation, these gifts were not given for the sake of the disciple. God did not save His people and then seek to make them happy by blessing them with spiritual gifts. Salvation is for a purpose much larger than a person's happiness. Spiritual gifts and resources are the same. To think otherwise is to reveal a human-centric approach to salvation and God. In reality, all of God's actions point back to Him and His glory. The way a disciple uses his or her spiritual gifts must also be God-centric, meaning that they bring Him glory by serving others and reflecting His grace. Gifts are not for a disciple's own benefit but for God's glory in the way they are used to serve others.

How are you using your gifts for the sake of others? How are you being responsible with the stewardship of God's glory?

PRAYER
Heavenly Father, transform my mind so that all of my life is centered on You. Forgive me for the responsibilities I have shirked. Empower me to honor You by serving others. Amen.

USING GOD'S GIFTS WISELY
Week 18: *Gifted to Love*

WITH GOD'S STRENGTH
1 Peter 4:11a

If anyone speaks, they should do so as one who speaks the very words of God. If anyone serves, they should do so with the strength God provides, so that in all things God may be praised through Jesus Christ.

Peter laid out a lofty goal in this verse. He told his readers to speak the very words of God. Earlier he told them to love deeply and to serve others selflessly. None of these actions are easy. In fact, they are quite impossible for a Christian to do, no matter how strong-willed he or she is.

Peter knew this conundrum. He understood it well. The same man who had denied Jesus three times after following Him closely for three years understood all too well that being able to follow His commands was downright impossible in his own human strength. That's why Peter reminded his readers that they can only obey Him through the strength that God provides. God's given mission is to make disciples of all nations. God gives the gifts and resources needed to accomplish that mission. And then He gives His own strength through which a disciple is able to use those gifts to obey Him. He is, indeed, a God of details, love, and power. God did not give a mission and expect His people to do it on their own. He gave Himself—through His Son and through His Holy Spirit. It is through this power alone that believers can be faithful stewards of all that God has entrusted to them.

How does it make you feel when you have been trying to obey God in your own strength? Why is it freeing to realize that you don't have to do so? Respond below.

PRAYER
Heavenly Father, I admit that I cannot follow or obey You in my own power. Fill me with Your strength so that You can live through me. Amen.

USING GOD'S GIFTS WISELY
Week 18: *Gifted to Love*
FOR GOD'S GLORY   1 Peter 4:11b

To him be the glory and the power for ever and ever. Amen.

Peter concluded this passage with a summary statement about why everything he had just written was important. The reason that a believer does anything is so that God may be glorified. When disciples are part of God's mission, worship happens as people come to praise the name of Jesus and the salvation He offers. Everything is about worship and mission.

The final point of stewardship is not about not wasting time on social media, handling money well, or being confident in a spiritual gift. It's about the glory of God and making Him known to all peoples. Being a good steward is about being responsible caretakers of what God has provided so that His people can be a part of accomplishing God's mission of reaching all nations. A disciple's motivation is God's glory. A disciple's goal is God's glory. A disciple's purpose is God's glory. And that is the reason for stewardship.

Respond to these questions below: How does your view of stewardship change when you realize the grand purpose and picture of it? How have your priorities changed as you have journeyed through these weeks discussing the gravity of what you have been entrusted with?

PRAYER
Heavenly Father, continually bring to mind the purpose of my life and my obedience to You. Amen.

_____

_____

_____

_____

_____

ACTING OUT FAITH
Week 19: *Growing Faith*

JOY IN TRIAL
James 1:2–4

Consider it pure joy, my brothers and sisters, whenever you face trials of many kinds, because you know that the testing of your faith produces perseverance. Let perseverance finish its work so that you may be mature and complete, not lacking anything.

Master chess players understand that they do not play the board as they see it in the present. A chess master anticipates several moves ahead and weighs the implications of his and his opponent's moves. As a result, a given move may seem counter-productive or harmful to the master, but the master has a greater goal in mind.

In this way, the Father is similar to the master chess player. He allows His children to undergo trials that may seem harmful or pointless when isolated from His greater purpose. However, a time will come when the scope of the Father's plan will be revealed and its brilliance will be breathtaking. Oftentimes we can see how God used difficult times to produce something good in our lives after a trial has passed. Time and perspective make God's purpose in difficult times clear.

Think about trials that you have faced. How has the Lord used difficult circumstances to produce good things? Use the space below to record your responses.

PRAYER
Heavenly Father, thank You for how You have shaped me through difficult circumstances. Help me to remember Your goodness in my struggles. Amen.

ACTING OUT FAITH
Week 19: *Growing Faith*

SIGNIFICANCE IN SUFFERING — James 1:12

Blessed is the one who perseveres under trial because, having stood the test, that person will receive the crown of life that the Lord has promised to those who love him.

Trials are trials for a reason—they typically aren't pleasant. There are times when abandoning one's faith can seem especially tempting under especially difficult trials. One may reason, "If my faith has brought me this trouble, it would be easier to abandon my faith."

However, perseverance under trial results in the affirmation and blessing of God. Imagine, one day, after you have persevered through all the trials of your life, God will crown them with significance by giving you "the crown of life." This knowledge fills otherwise painful experiences with great joy and significance. The God of the universe notices your afflictions and will personally reward you with the crown of life when you remain steadfast under trial.

Remember, God's love for you crowns your trials with great significance. Below, list some of the trials you're experiencing right now. How is God directing you through these trials?

PRAYER
Father, help me to remember the reward you promise for me when I persevere under trials. Thank you for the truth that you give my struggles significance. Amen.

_____

_____

_____

_____

ACTING OUT FAITH
Week 19: *Growing Faith*
GOD, GOODNESS, AND TEMPTATION   James 1:13

When tempted, no one should say, "God is tempting me." For God cannot be tempted by evil, nor does he tempt anyone.

God can be trusted in temptation because He is completely good. No evil can be found in the character of God so He can be trusted completely when we experience temptations and trials. As a result, turning to God as our refuge in temptation means we are able to resist the temptation to give in to sin.

When tempted to sin, we should commit ourselves to pursuing God and remembering His goodness. God is not the source of evil and never desires for His children to come under the consequences of sin. Pursuing the goodness of God in the midst of a temptation is a way to re-orient our minds and desires that can easily be manipulated to pursue evil. Pursuing God intentionally sets our hearts and minds on pursuing righteousness and re-boots our systems to run the way God intended.

How does God's goodness motivate you to resist temptation? Respond below and then thank God for His presence in your life.

PRAYER
Heavenly Father, thank You that You are all good and that temptation does not come from You. Help me to remember Your goodness when I am tempted. Amen.

_____

_____

_____

_____

_____

ACTING OUT FAITH
Week 19: *Growing Faith*
A SLIPPERY SLOPE
James 1:14–15

But each person is tempted when they are dragged away by their own evil desire and enticed. Then, after desire has conceived, it gives birth to sin; and sin, when it is full-grown, gives birth to death.

Since God is not the source of temptation, what is? James' answer is clear: an individual's desire. We are prone to enticement for things that appear good and satisfying to ourselves and we quickly forget that God Himself is the greatest good we can obtain.

Instead of pursuing God, we become distracted by things that are less than His best for us. We desire joy and fulfillment but we allow ourselves to be persuaded that something outside of God Himself can fulfill our deepest longings. All we see is the bright, shiny temptation that falsely promises to solve all our problems, and give us contentment, or at least temporary relief, from our situation. Unfortunately for us, the result of pursuing less than God Himself leads us into the arms of sin and sin leads to death. We almost never see this initially.

Giving in to temptation may provide momentary relief, but our troubles are only compounded as sin takes further grip on our lives. Have you experienced the fruit of selfishly seeking your own satisfaction? How has God rescued you from yourself? Respond below.

PRAYER
Father, forgive me for the times that I give in to my own selfish desire. Help me to pursue Your best for my life in all circumstances. Amen.

ACTING OUT FAITH
Week 19: *Growing Faith*

TRUE NORTH
James 1:16–17

Don't be deceived, my dear brothers and sisters. Every good and perfect gift is from above, coming down from the Father of the heavenly lights, who does not change like shifting shadows.

Ancient naval navigators determined how they could return to their homeports by identifying the port's angle to the North Star. No matter where in the world they were, navigators only had to identify the North Star, set sail north or south, and line the ship up in the same angle at which their homeport was located to return home.

Because God's character is constant, He provides a "true north" by which believers can navigate trials and temptations. No situation changes God, so God and His revealed truth provide a fixed point by which believers can orient their lives and priorities. No matter the circumstances in which we find ourselves, we only need to identify God's timeless truth and unwavering character in order to find our way.

How have you experienced the blessing of orienting yourself to God's truth in the midst of trials? Record your experiences below.

PRAYER
Heavenly Father, thank You that You are constant in my trials and tribulations. Help me to keep myself grounded in Your truth at all times. Amen.

_____

_____

_____

_____

_____

ACTING OUT FAITH
Week 20: *Integrated Faith*

OUT WITH THE OLD — James 1:21a

Therefore, get rid of all moral filth and the evil that is so prevalent...

Coming to Christ means changes in lifestyle. For some of us, these changes are obvious. Formerly, you may have been addicted to a destructive substance or behavior and Christ gave you freedom. Testimonies such as these are powerful and give evidence to the greatness and sufficiency of Christ. Others may not have such a "powerful" testimony, but the fact that Christ saves any of us from our sin, no matter how obvious the sin, is still a powerful testimony.

Coming to Christ does not guarantee that we will no longer struggle with any sin. However, we are instructed to continue to put away anything that characterizes our old style of life. Any sin, no matter how small it may seem, is in direct opposition for God's will for his children. Sin stains us; Christ desires for us to be washed clean of all the filthiness of sin.

Is there any sin with which you still struggle from which you need Christ to cleanse you? Give that over to Christ and record below your feelings of asking Christ for help.

PRAYER
Father, thank You for saving me from my sin. Help me to continue to put away anything that characterizes my old life apart from You. Amen.

ACTING OUT FAITH
Week 20: *Integrated Faith*

FROM THE INSIDE OUT

James 1:21b

...And humbly accept the word planted in you, which can save you.

God knows that behavior modification is simply insufficient to fix mankind's incessant need to pursue sin and experience death. Conformity to external rules, laws, and codes does not fix our heart issue. We can obey all the rules and our hearts can still be resistant and hard towards our Creator.

God's purpose in Christ is to create a new sort of person—one who is made new through "the implanted word." This is one of the great mysteries of the Christian faith. Upon professing your faith in Christ, Christ takes up residence in your heart and replaces your heart of stone, one characterized by resisting and rebelling against God, with a heart of flesh that is receptive and open to God's leading in your life. It is only by allowing Christ to perform this work, to implant the word in our hearts, that we are saved.

Any change in our behavior after we profess faith in Christ stems from the reality of a changed heart and the indwelling Christ in us. Prayerfully consider how your heart reflects Christ's word. Below, record where you want your heart to be in your relationship with Christ.

PRAYER
Heavenly Father, thank You for changing my heart and living in me. Amen.

_____

_____

_____

_____

_____

_____

_____

ACTING OUT FAITH
Week 20: *Integrated Faith*
SELF-DECEPTION James 1:22

Do not merely listen to the word, and so deceive yourselves. Do what it says.

Christian faith is sometimes equated with adherence to a set of doctrines and principles. If one believes the right things, that person is said to be a Christian. In this understanding of faith, action is minimized and faith is all in one's head. However, James spoke strongly against this understanding of Christian faith.

Simply put, understanding faith as only a set of ideas or facts is false. James went so far as to say that if one takes no action in response to the faith they hear about and profess, they have deceived themselves. Faith was never meant to remain in the realm of ideas or abstract principles. Authentic faith in Christ produces action and obedience to the word that has been implanted in us. Inward realities produce outward action.

Below, respond to these questions: How has your faith resulted in action in your life? Do you need to repent of the self-deception of minimizing your response to what you profess to believe?

PRAYER
Father, thank You for transforming me in Christ. Show me how You desire for me to live my faith. Amen.

ACTING OUT FAITH
Week 20: *Integrated Faith*
FAITH AND FOLLY
James 1:23-24

Anyone who listens to the word but does not do what it says is like someone who looks at his face in a mirror and, after looking at himself, goes away and immediately forgets what he looks like.

According to *Science Daily*, Americans spend a little over 40 minutes a day on personal grooming tasks like brushing our hair, applying make-up, or shaving. Imagine how useless these tasks would be if we immediately walked away and couldn't remember the result they produced. Who would continue to spend that much time doing something that apparently mattered so little?

For James, the very idea that one's beliefs would not work themselves out in how he or she lived would be as ludicrous as spending 40 minutes grooming yourself and not remembering how you looked afterwards. Spending all of one's time acquiring facts that do not produce action amounts to nothing. Authentic faith must produce action and not just intellectual agreement.

· What action does the Lord want your faith to produce?

PRAYER
Father, help me to understand how my professed faith in You affects how I live every day. Amen.

ACTING OUT FAITH
Week 20: *Integrated Faith*
THE SECRET OF BLESSING James 1:25

But whoever looks intently into the perfect law that gives freedom, and continues in it—not forgetting what they have heard, but doing it—they will be blessed in what they do.

We exert so much effort and emotional anguish attempting to discern God's will for our lives. Such a desire is rightly placed. For God's children to desire to be found in obedience to His will is proper and is certainly commendable. But the secret to God's blessing in our lives isn't only found in one day being in the right place, or job, or situation.

Instead, the secret of living in God's blessing is to understand how God desires for His children to conduct themselves in the particularities of daily life and then living according to His ways. God's children are promised His blessing, but not when they finally reach a place of God's blessing. Instead, God's children are promised God's blessing when they live lives that prove they are His children every day by their obedience to what they already know. We look forward to God acting on our behalf and more fully revealing His will for us, but we do not wait for this to happen before we live as his children.

Are you neglecting any aspect of living as God's child in your present situation?

PRAYER
Heavenly Father, thank You that You have a plan for me. Help me to live as Your child as I wait for that plan to be fully revealed. Amen.

ACTING OUT FAITH
Week 21: *Pure and Undefiled Faith*
HOW TO DECEIVE YOURSELF
James 1:26a

Those who consider themselves religious and yet do not keep a tight rein on their tongues deceive themselves...

English philosopher Francis Bacon said, "Man prefers to believe what he prefers to be true." In the case of their spiritual life, people typically like to ascribe higher levels of spirituality to themselves than are actually true. We want to feel like we are close to God, that we represent Christ better than we do, and that we love our neighbors as we love ourselves even though evidence to the fact is lacking.

Unfortunately, when we apply biblical standards of what it means to live faith practically in Christ, we tend to make excuses rather than prayers of repentance. We love God and want to live according to His truths. But for many of us, ten minutes a day to read the Bible is just too much with our busy schedules. We want to share Christ with our friend, but he or she may think we're weird. We want to love our neighbor, but he or she is really annoying. Surely, we tell ourselves, Jesus understands.

What areas of disobedience do you recognize in your own life? How have you rationalized these areas? Respond below.

PRAYER
Heavenly Father, forgive me for when I make excuses rather than obey Your word. Help me to live my faith today. Amen.

ACTING OUT FAITH
Week 21: *Pure and Undefiled Faith*
HOW TO HAVE WORTHLESS FAITH   James 1:26

Those who consider themselves religious and yet do not keep a tight rein on their tongues deceive themselves, and their religion is worthless.

Bridles are the headgear and mouth bits by which riders control the direction of a horse. They are relatively small compared to the horse, but they exercise great control over the horse's direction. Without a bridle, controlling the direction of the horse, especially a stubborn one, is very difficult.

In the same way that a small bridle carries tremendous influence on a large horse, the tongue—a relatively small appendage—has great capacity to influence the direction of a person. Careless words spoken at a moment of vulnerability can cause immeasurable damage to another person. Living one's faith in Christ should mean learning to keep one's tongue under control. Careless words spoken in anger or ignorance can do tremendous damage to your witness and the cause of Christ.

How will you keep a bridle on your tongue to only speak uplifting words? Respond below.

PRAYER
Heavenly Father, thank You that You give me the means I need to control my tongue. Help me to use my tongue to build others up and to testify to Your greatness. Amen.

_____

_____

_____

_____

_____

_____

ACTING OUT FAITH
Week 21: *Pure and Undefiled Faith*

HOW TO DECEIVE YOUR HEART
James 1:26

Those who consider themselves religious and yet do not keep a tight rein on their tongues deceive themselves, and their religion is worthless.

Lack of constraint of one's tongue points to a much larger issue than occasionally letting careless words fly. The inability to keep one's tongue restrained points deep within a person. Flying off the handle is not a flippant, quirky, character trait. When a follower of Christ can't help but let some choice words fly, a heart issue is always involved.

Making light of your inability to restrain your words is symptomatic of a heart that has allowed itself to be convinced that it is better off than it is. When we allow ourselves to spout off at the slightest irritation, when we really want to let someone have it regardless of whether they deserve it or not, we demonstrate that we have allowed our hearts to become puffed up in our estimation of ourselves.

Think back over the words you have spoken over the last 24 hours. Is there evidence of a heart that has been deceived? Respond below.

PRAYER
Heavenly Father, forgive me for the times I deceive my heart by what I allow to come out of my mouth. Amen.

_____

_____

_____

_____

_____

_____

_____

ACTING OUT FAITH
Week 21: *Pure and Undefiled Faith*
HOW TO HAVE PURE FAITH, PART 1   James 1:27

Religion that God our Father accepts as pure and faultless is this: to look after orphans and widows in their distress and to keep oneself from being polluted by the world.

A lot has been said about how we allow ourselves to be deceived in regards to our faith in Christ. How, then, can we know if our faith has made an impact on our lives in a practical sense? One of the easiest tests is to see how our faith impacts the way we care for others, particularly those who often lack the means to care for themselves.

Two such populations of individuals for whom Christians should show special care are orphans and widows. Why orphans and widows? They are two groups that often get thrown aside and forgotten in our society because of their misfortune. These individuals can often feel abandoned or forgotten by God without someone intervening in their situation and showing them love. Christians are exhorted to stand in this gap and demonstrate that God has not, in fact, forgotten about them.

Is there someone in your life to whom you need to demonstrate the love of Christ? Who would that be and what actions do you need to take? Respond below.

PRAYER
Heavenly Father, help me to represent You well to those who feel like You have abandoned them. Amen.

_____

_____

_____

_____

_____

ACTING OUT FAITH
Week 21: *Pure and Undefiled Faith*
HOW TO HAVE PURE FAITH, PART 2   James 1:27

Religion that God our Father accepts as pure and faultless is this: to look after orphans and widows in their distress and to keep oneself from being polluted by the world.

Have you ever told yourself, "It's only natural." Typically, we say or think this phrase when we are attempting to justify a behavior that, deep down, we know is unacceptable. Instead of repenting, we rationalize and assure ourselves that Jesus will understand. We allow our hearts to be deceived and we do not live as children of the Father.

A second standard of the efficacy of a believer's faith is offered here. One's relationship with Christ should evidence itself in his or her willingness to care for those for whom no one else has cared. It should also lead the believer to abandon any worldly pattern of behavior, priorities, or thinking. The phrase, "It's only natural," should never depart from a believer's lips. As children of Christ, we are called to transcend what is natural. What is natural leads to spiritual death; Christ makes us alive.

Do you need to repent of any "natural" behavior that is unfit for a child of the Father? Take that to the Father.

PRAYER
Heavenly Father, forgive me for the times I allow myself to be influenced by the standards of the world. Help me to be found faithful according to Your standards. Amen.

ACTING OUT FAITH
Week 22: *Obedient Faith*

DEAD FAITH
James 2:14–17

What good is it, my brothers and sisters, if someone claims to have faith but has no deeds? Can such faith save them? Suppose a brother or a sister is without clothes and daily food. If one of you says to them, "Go in peace; keep warm and well fed," but does nothing about their physical needs, what good is it? In the same way, faith by itself, if it is not accompanied by action, is dead.

Assuring others of our prayers for them has become the Christian thing to do for needs that seem too difficult for us to personally meet. Praying for brothers and sisters is a great thing to do, and a discipline that we should regularly practice. However, there are times when assuring our prayers for a brother or sister is a cop-out to taking any action to provide immediate assistance.

Such assistance can be costly. It interrupts our schedule, blows up our budget, and generally, can result in an awkward experience as you provide for someone to whom you would not typically relate. Such assistance is also a measuring stick for authentic faith. If our faith in Christ motivates us to nothing more than expressing spiritual platitudes when faced with a pressing need that we have the means to sacrificially meet, our faith is worthless and dead.

What interruptions in your life might God be allowing for you to put your faith into practice? Are there any immediate needs that you could sacrificially meet? Respond below.

PRAYER
Heavenly Father, help me to discern when You are providing an opportunity for me to sacrificially minister to a brother or sister. Amen.

_____

_____

_____

_____

ACTING OUT FAITH
Week 22: *Obedient Faith*
PROOF OF FAITH   James 2:18

But someone will say, "You have faith; I have deeds."

James continued to attack the idea that faith is only intellectual ascent to a series of statements, doctrines, principles, and ideas. Such a faith can remain remote and unengaged with the world. Faith in Christ is of a different sort. Faith in Christ is certainly the understanding and acceptance of a series of statements, doctrines, principles, and ideas. But faith in Christ engages the real world and not just the mind.

Faith in Christ leads to good works. Good works are the practical demonstration of one's inner faith that seeks to model the example of our Savior. Christ, being God, took on human flesh and engaged in the world. He did not remain in the realm of ideas alone. We are to follow His example and demonstrate that we have been redeemed and renewed from the inside out. For us, this means that we perform good works as a testimony to the inward nature of our transformation. A lack of good works demonstrates a lack of authentic faith.

Prayerfully consider what good work the Lord has set before you to perform today. Then, respond below.

PRAYER
Heavenly Father, help me to testify to the total transformation of my inward nature through the good works I perform today. Amen.

ACTING OUT FAITH
Week 22: *Obedient Faith*
DEMONIC FAITH
James 2:19

You believe that there is one God. Good! Even the demons believe that—and shudder.

As further proof that understanding a set of ideas does not equate to true faith in Christ, James offered one of the most startling statements in all of Scripture. The members of James' original audience were most likely Christians from a Jewish background. As former Jews, one of the central attestations of faith was the Shema: "Hear, oh Israel, the Lord your God, the Lord is one." (Deuteronomy 6:4). Belief in the one true God was central both to their former faith and their current faith in Jesus.

An individual who rests simply on professing faith in the existence of God keeps unlikely company. Even demons believe all the right things about God. They believe that He is one. They know He is omniscient and omnipotent. They even have the ability to wax poetic about the intricacies of Calvinism and Arminianism. However, demons are still damned. Their level of knowledge has not saved them. Though they know all the right things, their natures are opposed to God. Demons are proof that knowing the correct things about God can result in a faith that does not save.

Reflect on your faith. Does your life demonstrate your belief in God? Are you ever guilty of professing faith through ideas and not actions? Respond below.

PRAYER
Heavenly Father, help me to live my faith and not allow it to remain in the realm of ideas. Amen.

ACTING OUT FAITH
Week 22: *Obedient Faith*
RISKY FAITH
James 2:20-25

You foolish person, do you want evidence that faith without deeds is useless? Was not our father Abraham considered righteous for what he did when he offered his son Isaac on the altar? You see that his faith and his actions were working together, and his faith was made complete by what he did. And the scripture was fulfilled that says, "Abraham believed God, and it was credited to him as righteousness," and he was called God's friend. You see that a person is considered righteous by what they do and not by faith alone. In the same way, was not even Rahab the prostitute considered righteous for what she did when she gave lodging to the spies and sent them off in a different direction?

Works are the means by which faith is demonstrated. They are the outward expression of an inward reality. Faith and works always go hand in hand. Abraham believed that God would fulfill His promise to make his descendants as numerous as the stars in the sky. He believed God's promise so completely that he was willing to obey God's command to sacrifice the son for whom he had waited for thirty years. Abraham believed that if he obeyed God, God would somehow still fulfill His promise even though Abraham couldn't see how.

Similarly, Rahab the prostitute's faith was demonstrated by her willingness to house Jewish spies in her home on their mission to scout Jericho. Rahab risked a charge of treason under which she and her entire family could be executed because she had faith in a God about whom she had only heard. She trusted that God was powerful enough to give His people victory and powerful enough to care for her.

In many ways, Abraham and Rahab could not be more different. However, they both demonstrated their faith in God by taking tremendous risk and trusting Him for the result.

PRAYER
Heavenly Father, help me to trust You in faith when You call me to take risks in Your name. Amen.

ACTING OUT FAITH
Week 22: *Obedient Faith*

TRUTH TESTING James 2:24, 26

You see that a person is considered righteous by what they do and not by faith alone...As the body without the spirit is dead, so faith without deeds is dead.

Faith and works go hand in hand. Remove faith and the foundation for works is removed. What is the motivation? Remove works and the efficacy of faith is abandoned. What good is faith if it does not promote action? Faith and works are inseparable and must go together.

Faith encourages an individual to take action. Once action is taken, the authenticity of faith is displayed. As believers, we were convicted by the Spirit but then took action to pray a prayer of repentance. As a next step in our faith, we were encouraged to be baptized. As we continue to deepen in our understanding of faith in Christ, the Spirit guides us to continue to take actions to put legs to our faith. Removing one element of the balance between faith and works upsets the entire process and results in dead faith.

What practical actions is the Lord leading you to take to put action to your faith? Write your response below.

PRAYER
Heavenly Father, help me to continue to put action to my faith as You lead me. Amen.

ACTING OUT FAITH
Week 23: *Verbal Faith*

A COMMON PROBLEM
James 3:2

We all stumble in many ways. Anyone who is never at fault in what they say is perfect, able to keep their whole body in check.

Placing our faith in Christ is, unfortunately, not a magic pill that forever solves our struggles with sin. We are still humans who still have a nature that wants to assert our own way over God's way. Christ in us begins to transform us through the process of sanctification, but as long as we are on this earth, we will each have our own struggles with various types of sin.

One particular vice with which everyone seems to struggle is our propensity to speak harmful or careless words. Our tongues can get us in a lot of trouble and are often the best demonstration of what is in our hearts. When we are frustrated, we are more likely to make a cutting remark. When we miss out on an opportunity, we are more likely to speak words questioning God's goodness or plan for our lives. The pervasive nature of humanity's problem with our tongues is summarized by James: If you can control your tongue, you can control anything and you are perfect! This does not excuse allowing our tongues to run amuck. It simply speaks to the difficulty of taming the tongue.

What steps do you need to take to begin to reign in your tongue? Respond below.

PRAYER
Heavenly Father, forgive me for harmful or careless words I have spoken. Help me to learn to control my tongue. Amen.

ACTING OUT FAITH
Week 23: *Verbal Faith*
SMALL BUT POWERFUL
James 3:3–5a

When we put bits into the mouths of horses to make them obey us, we can turn the whole animal. Or take ships as an example. Although they are so large and are driven by strong winds, they are steered by a very small rudder wherever the pilot wants to go. Likewise, the tongue is a small part of the body, but it makes great boasts.

The modern proverb is certainly true: dynamite does come in small packages! Small things often have the potential to wield great influence. A bit in the mouth of a horse is small in comparison to the horse itself, but allows a rider to exert great control over the direction of a horse. A large ship has its sails filled by the wind, but its course is changed by a rudder that is roughly 1/70th the ship's size.

Yet look at the effect that these relatively small things have on objects much greater than themselves! Without a bit in its mouth, a stubborn horse can give its rider many problems. Without a small rudder, a ship would be unable to make any course corrections. A bit in the mouth of a horse and a rudder on a ship reign in the power of two great objects and enable them to be useful, not simply powerful or majestic. So, too, reigning in one's tongue enables a person to utilize a great power for a good purpose.

What do you need to do today to help you control your tongue better?

PRAYER
Heavenly Father, thank You for the opportunity You have given me to use my words for good and not for harm. Amen.

ACTING OUT FAITH
Week 23: *Verbal Faith*
SMALL BEGINNINGS James 3:5b–6

Consider what a great forest is set on fire by a small spark. The tongue also is a fire, a world of evil among the parts of the body. It corrupts the whole body, sets the whole course of one's life on fire, and is itself set on fire by hell.

While our tongues have the capacity to do great good to and for others, more often than not the power of the tongue is demonstrated by its capacity to destroy. Just as a small forest fire can eventually spread to destroy an entire forest, the tongue's destructive effects can begin small but, if left unchecked, have a tremendous destructive capacity. Our tongues are generally the most reliable testimony of our nearness to the Father. When we have allowed ourselves to become a verbal "fire," our tongues become more destructive and betray the true state of our heart.

Just as a spark in a forest can ignite under the right conditions, careless words spoken from an un-kept heart have the potential to ignite our lives into chaos. Emotional, psychological, spiritual, and relational turmoil can all be instigated through the power of our tongues. Before we even realize it, the consequences of a careless word can be on us and cause unmitigated damage that will take much more time to repair than it did to cause. James noted that the destructive capabilities of our words are empowered by hell itself.

Have you experienced the negative consequences of your words? How can you prevent this from happening again? Respond below.

PRAYER
Heavenly Father, forgive me for when I use my words to harm others and myself. Amen.

ACTING OUT FAITH
Week 23: *Verbal Faith*

INCOMPATIBLE

James 3:8–10

But no human being can tame the tongue. It is a restless evil, full of deadly poison. With the tongue we praise our Lord and Father, and with it we curse human beings, who have been made in God's likeness. Out of the same mouth come praise and cursing. My brothers and sisters, this should not be.

Even after coming to Christ, believers will still struggle with sin. This is no more evident than in our constant struggle with our tongues. For anyone to have a complete reign on their tongue at all times, in all circumstances, seems impossible. Popping off a cutting remark, expressing a veiled criticism, and insulting another under the guise of a joke sometimes just seems to come out.

As believers, our tongues often make us hypocrites. We love to sing about the greatness of our God and to speak of the hope that we have in Christ, and in the next minute tear down a brother or sister with our words. We love to praise and we love to speak ill. The behaviors are incompatible, so one must be eliminated. To sing praises and to tell of the greatness of Christ are certainly things that God wants us to do. We are then left with abandoning our negative comments and criticisms about those who have been made in God's image. The very idea of praising God but speaking ill of those who bear His image is ludicrous when we stop and think about it. In effect, we are saying, "We love the Creator for who He is but who He is could have produced a better product."

Do your words about others reflect your belief about God? Why? Do you have work to do in this area of your life? Respond below.

PRAYER
Heavenly Father, help me to strive to only speak words of blessing today. Amen.

_____
_____
_____

ACTING OUT FAITH
Week 23: *Verbal Faith*
THE PRODUCT AND THE SOURCE James 3:11–12

Can both fresh water and salt water flow from the same spring? My brothers and sisters, can a fig tree bear olives, or a grapevine bear figs? Neither can a salt spring produce fresh water.

"If it looks like a duck, walks like a duck, and quacks like a duck, it's probably a duck." The logic of this statement is obvious. If an animal has all the products, properties, behaviors, and appearances of a duck, to label it as an eagle, a rhinoceros, or a humpback whale would be equally ridiculous. Of course it's not one of those things! It's a duck!

When it comes to observing our behavior, we tend to excuse obvious parallels between observations about our actions and what those observations say about their source. When we speak an angry word with someone, it's not because there is anger stored up in our heart—it's because they did something that justified our angry response. When we make a cutting criticism of someone's appearance, it's not because we feel defensive and somewhat insecure today—it's because they should just know that whatever they did is not in good taste or downright offensive. In response, James wrote that salt ponds cannot produce fresh water. A heart at rest and at peace with God does not produce angry or cutting remarks.

What do the words you have spoken in the last 24 hours say about the condition of your heart right now? Respond below.

PRAYER
Heavenly Father, help me to keep my heart in fellowship with You. Amen.

ACTING OUT FAITH
Week 24: *Imitated Faith*

FROM WITHIN

James 4:1–2a

What causes fights and quarrels among you? Don't they come from your desires that battle within you? You desire but do not have, so you kill. You covet but you cannot get what you want, so you quarrel and fight.

It has been said that when we point a finger at someone else, we point three back at ourselves. Our problem is that we tend to minimize our own role in our misbehavior and sins. Since Adam and Eve, passing the buck for sin has been the game of humanity. Whether we honestly think we are not culpable, or if it simply a gut-level reaction, is irrelevant. The practical result is the same: we minimize personal responsibility and locate blame on others or in circumstances.

James showed that responsibility for interpersonal conflicts rest squarely on an individual's misplaced passions. When we focus our attention and effort on objects outside of the Father and substitute desire for the creation over desire for the Creator, interpersonal conflict results. Our misplaced passions result in sinful actions. The problem is not that we were provoked and our actions are therefore excusable. The problem is that our desire has been misplaced and resulted in sin. The problem is not external; it is internal.

Are there issues in any of your interpersonal relationships? Examine your heart before you point a finger and then record your thoughts below.

PRAYER
Heavenly Father, help me to see how misplaced passions have affected my relationships. Amen.

ACTING OUT FAITH
Week 24: *Imitated Faith*

A TWO-PRONGED PROBLEM
James 4:2b–3

You do not have because you do not ask God. When you ask, you do not receive, because you ask with wrong motives, that you may spend what you get on your pleasures.

Chief among humanity's main vices is our hard-hearted stubbornness that refuses to acknowledge our dependence on anything outside of ourselves. And second is our extreme selfishness that evaluates all of life's events on the impact that it has on us personally, as if the whole of history has culminated in our existence. On the one hand, we refuse to acknowledge God because doing so is to admit that we are not completely self-sufficient. We are, in fact, dependent on God. On the other hand, our selfishness clouds our perception. Though we admit dependence on God and petition Him for something, we do so from a heart that seeks to satisfy our wants, needs, and passions above all else.

James roundly condemned both attitudes as unbecoming of Christian prayer. We are not completely self-sufficient and we do depend on God to sustain every aspect of our lives. Our prayers should reflect and acknowledge this understanding. When we make petitions of God, we should only expect to receive His blessings when our desires and passions align with His. God is not to be treated as a cosmic genie who will bend to our every whim. Instead, prayer should be an exercise in bending our will to His and aligning our desires with His. God is not obligated to answer self-centered and self-exalting prayer.

Do your prayers, or lack thereof, reflect either of these attitudes? Respond below.

PRAYER
Heavenly Father, forgive me for my stubbornness in not coming to You and my selfishness in the attitude in which I come to You. Amen.

ACTING OUT FAITH
Week 24: *Imitated Faith*

RIGHTEOUS JEALOUSY James 4:4–6a

You adulterous people, don't you know that friendship with the world means enmity against God? Therefore, anyone who chooses to be a friend of the world becomes an enemy of God. Or do you think Scripture says without reason that he jealously longs for the spirit he has caused to dwell in us? But he gives us more grace.

My sisters always knew how to get under my skin growing up. All they had to do was "borrow" something of mine and not let me know about it. I would go looking for it, find that they had it without asking, and an argument always ensued. My incessant plea was constant: "But it's mine!"

Selfish motivations aside, my childhood longing reflects God's attitude towards humanity. He created us in His image. We are His. Yet we allow the bright and shiny things of the world to distract us. We buy into the lies that the things of the world can satisfy us, or that the answer to our deepest troubles is to pursue what makes us happy, or anything that locates purpose in a relationship with our Creator. In pursuing these things, we buy in to the worldly system of resistance to the Creator God and we make ourselves "an enemy of God." Instead of rightly submitting ourselves to God, we locate ourselves in the way of the world characterized by sin and rebellion against God.

We are created in God's image for His pleasure and purpose. He longs for us to be in a right relationship with Him. Prayerfully reflect on your relationship with God. Is it in a right relationship? Why? Respond below.

PRAYER
Heavenly Father, show me any way that I have made friends with the world and pushed Your ways to the side. Amen.

_____

_____

_____

_____

ACTING OUT FAITH
Week 24: *Imitated Faith*
THE PROBLEM OF PRIDE
James 4:6b–8a

That is why Scripture says: "God opposes the proud but shows favor to the humble." Submit yourselves, then, to God. Resist the devil, and he will flee from you. Come near to God and he will come near to you.

Imagine a hypothetical situation in which there are two options. If we choose option 1, God will support us; if we choose option 2, God will oppose us. If we could know beyond a shadow of a doubt the possibility of those two options, we would be certifiably insane to choose option 2. However, we are making this choice any time we routinely choose option 2 — the way of pride. Acting, speaking, or thinking out of pride is the best way to ensure that God will oppose us. And it is Satan's favorite tool for trapping us in the consequences and repercussions of our sin. God promises to oppose our pride. Yet, we persist in acting out of it.

Do not miss the crucial connection James made in these verses. We are tempted to isolate sentences but we do so to our detriment. God opposes the proud but gives grace to the humble. Submission to God, therefore, equals adopting an attitude of humility. Resisting the devil is synonymous with resisting the temptation of pride that invokes the opposition of God. When we adopt an attitude of humility, we are adopting the attitude of God. In so doing, we make a step towards our Creator and He has promised to meet us in that step. Resolving to adopt an attitude of humility is the secret to intimacy with God and enmity with Satan because it resolves the core problem of most of our sin: our battle with pride.

Are there any elements of pride in your life that are hindering your intimacy with God? Confess those below and then give them over to God.

PRAYER
Heavenly Father, forgive me for my pride. Help me to live a life of humble communion with You. Amen.

ACTING OUT FAITH
Week 24: *Imitated Faith*
A HOLY MELANCHOLY
James 4:8b–10

Wash your hands, you sinners, and purify your hearts, you double-minded. Grieve, mourn and wail. Change your laughter to mourning and your joy to gloom. Humble yourselves before the Lord, and he will lift you up.

James' prescription for intimacy with God does not jive with our conceptions of a meaningful worship experience! We value celebration and we desire to elevate those who attend our gatherings. We want to assure them of God's presence and love for them. We want to build them up and provide a good experience in order to keep them coming back for more.

While these desires are good, there are times when it is appropriate for us to come before God in a repentant posture. We must never portray God as a kindly grandfather figure who approves of us no matter what we do to the detriment of His holiness that demanded a payment for our sin. At times, it is appropriate for us to come before God penitently, keenly aware of the cost of our sin. Sometimes it is appropriate for us to approach God in a posture of mourning as we become aware of the price of our sin and, ultimately, how our sin led to the sacrifice of God's son. When we remember the reality of our sin and our powerlessness to solve our sin problem on our own, we are driven to an attitude of humility.

When we can acknowledge the reality of our sin and express an honest, repentant attitude towards it, God promises to exalt us. Spend the next minutes in prayer as you meditate on this last statement. Then, record your experience below.

PRAYER
Heavenly Father, remind me of how much I have been forgiven today. Help the memory of my sin drive me to humility before You. Amen.

_____

_____

_____

_____

COMING BACK TO GOD
Week 25: *Confess Sin*

A COSTLY GRACE
Psalm 51:1

Have mercy on me, O God, according to your unfailing love; according to your great compassion blot out my transgressions.

The simple request that begins this psalm doesn't give much clue to the heartbreaking tale of deception and murder behind it. The psalmist David took a long journey to get to this point of repentance and, in the end, he paid a great price. His plea for forgiveness came from a heart broken by bitter sorrow.

In today's culture, sorrow over sin is uncommon. Wrong is called right; moral failings are explained away. As our understanding of sin erodes, so goes our appreciation of forgiveness. Dietrich Bonhoeffer, the German pastor who died at the hands of the Nazis, indicted the church for peddling "cheap grace"—forgiveness without true repentance. He wrote, "Cheap grace means the justification of the sin without the justification of the sinner."

When we understand the seriousness of sin, we understand the cost of forgiveness. In the space below, consider the events recorded in 2 Samuel 11:1–12:23. Jot down your thoughts on how to prevent falling into sin like David.

PRAYER
Heavenly Father, help me remember that I could fall into sin as easily as David. Help me stay focused on You. Amen.

COMING BACK TO GOD
Week 25: *Confess Sin*

WHEN SIN CREEPS IN
Psalm 51:3

For I know my transgressions, and my sin is always before me.

Eighteenth century hymnwriter William Cowper worked and served alongside John Newton, the former slave trader who penned the hymn *Amazing Grace*. Though working with a vibrant preacher such as Newton might seem an inoculation against weak faith, Cowper found himself battling some old demons of depression and fear when a close friend and mother figure fell deathly ill.

Cowper prayed that the trial would have a sanctifying effect. As God brought his spiritual condition to mind, Cowper wrote the words to *O For a Closer Walk with God*. The third verse reads: "Return, O holy Dove, return, sweet messenger of rest! I hate the sins that made Thee mourn and drove Thee from my breast."

Sin weakens faith and gives doubt a platform by which believers are robbed of faith. Like Cowper and the psalmist David, ask God to reveal your spiritual condition to you. Jot down what God brings to mind.

PRAYER
Heavenly Father, forgive me for my pride. Help me to live a life of humble communion with You. Amen.

COMING BACK TO GOD
Week 25: *Confess Sin*

THE HIGH COST OF SIN Psalm 51:4

...you are right in your verdict and justified when you judge.

A young man in our church youth group lost his life when another teenager, inebriated and the same age as our friend, crashed through a red light while fleeing from police. On the witness stand at trial, the accused sobbed; his sentence was a mere one-year probation. The town was left feeling that justice had not been served.

Instinctively, we chaff when justice is not carried out. When wronged by others, we realize how difficult forgiveness can be. It is painful to let go of resentment, anger, and loss. It costs us something to forgive those that hurt us. M. C. D'Arcy wrote in *Death and Life*, "The astonishing revelation of Calvary is in part that man's actions are so gigantic and irreparable as to require the death of God himself to put them right."

Do you understand what it cost God to forgive you? Does this help you better understand the seriousness of your own sin? Respond below.

PRAYER
Heavenly Father, help me to understand the depth and seriousness of my sin. Help me understand what it cost You to offer forgiveness to me. Amen.

COMING BACK TO GOD
Week 25: *Confess Sin*

WHEN MERCY IS OFFERED   Psalm 51:9

Hide your face from my sins and blot out all my iniquity.

The youth minister sat in the pastor's office, admitting a secret that would rock the church. His affair with a married woman, a fellow seminary student, was ending his marriage as well as hers. "God will forgive us," was his only explanation. He showed no remorse and offered no regrets.

Andrew Murray in his book *Confession and Forgiveness* warned about those who bank on cheap grace: "They comfort themselves with the thought that God is merciful and have no idea that this of itself will avail them nothing....They forget that God is the righteous One as well as merciful and that before His righteousness can liberate a single soul, His holy law must be fulfilled." Mercy is offered only to the person who cries out to God for forgiveness and asks for a changed heart.

Use the space below to examine your own heart. Are you tempted to take your sin lightly? Are you tempted to overlook the sin of someone you admire because you think, "God will forgive"? Respond below.

PRAYER
Heavenly Father, forgive me for taking my sin and Your forgiveness too lightly. Show me any unconfessed sin my life. Amen.

COMING BACK TO GOD
Week 25: *Confess Sin*
HEART TRANSPLANT NEEDED   Psalm 51:10

Create in me a pure heart, O God, and renew a steadfast spirit within me.

For four generations, the same sin of anger and bitterness plagued a family in a story told by Philip Yancey in his book *What's So Amazing About Grace?* Though each new generation determined to act differently than the parent who had failed them, each unwittingly passed on to their offspring the cancer of unforgiveness that was ruining their lives.

Sin is serious. It has the power to imprison and maim. Only when we see ourselves as we really are can the cycle of sin that enslaves us be broken. We are not good people who simply make mistakes; we are corrupted at our core and need a new heart set in place by the Great Physician.

What bitterness, jealousy or self-centeredness are you holding onto? What past actions or thoughts keep you weighed down? Record your thoughts below.

PRAYER
Heavenly Father, show me my sin and help me to turn it over to You. Give me the steadfast spirit I need so I never slip back into that sin again. Amen.

COMING BACK TO GOD
Week 26: *Accept Consequences*

A GOD IN OUR IMAGE — Jonah 1:1-7

The word of the Lord came to Jonah son of Amittai: "Go to the great city of Nineveh and preach against it, because its wickedness has come up before me." But Jonah ran away from the Lord and headed for Tarshish. He went down to Joppa, where he found a ship bound for that port. After paying the fare, he went aboard and sailed for Tarshish to flee from the Lord. Then the Lord sent a great wind on the sea, and such a violent storm arose that the ship threatened to break up. All the sailors were afraid and each cried out to his own god. And they threw the cargo into the sea to lighten the ship. But Jonah had gone below deck, where he lay down and fell into a deep sleep. The captain went to him and said, "How can you sleep? Get up and call on your god! Maybe he will take notice of us so that we will not perish." Then the sailors said to each other, "Come, let us cast lots to find out who is responsible for this calamity." They cast lots and the lot fell on Jonah.

"Growing up in a judge's home wasn't easy," my husband likes to say. One thing was certain: whenever my husband's childhood antics required the attention of his father—the judge—there was no way to wiggle out.

"I hear better liars than you in court every day," my father-in-law would remind his young son. The disciplinary action handed down involved a written "sentence" with specifics for how the penalty would be worked off, plus the terms of "probation." My husband learned early that any stress to the father-son relationship caused by his disobedience was repaired quickly when he showed penitence. But consequences still had to be paid.

God disciplines us because He loves us. Accepting the consequences of our sin can help restore the Father-child relationship and make us confident of His character. In the space below, reflect on what God's discipline shows you about His nature.

PRAYER
Heavenly Father, help me remember that Your judgment is motivated by Your character. Thank You for loving me enough to discipline me. Amen.

COMING BACK TO GOD
Week 26: *Accept Consequences*

A CONFESSION, BUT SO WHAT? Jonah 1:8-10

So they asked him, "Tell us, who is responsible for making all this trouble for us? What kind of work do you do? Where do you come from? What is your country? From what people are you?" He answered, "I am a Hebrew and I worship the LORD, the God of heaven, who made the sea and the dry land." This terrified them and they asked, "What have you done?" (They knew he was running away from the LORD, because he had already told them so.)

"Character doesn't matter" became a part of America's persona sometime during the presidency of Bill Clinton and a second term tidal wave of moral failings, lying under oath, and impeachment. The nation groaned as embarrassing details of an admitted affair were made public in a legal firestorm that seemed unending. Clinton, and many supporters, made light of the lurid ordeal by insisting that personal sins "didn't matter."

Some hoped for Clinton's resignation if for no other reason than to end the daily news diet of scandal and sex. Nonetheless, Clinton fought back. Years later, at the release of a film about the ordeal, Clinton said, "The whole battle was a badge of honor." Though the nation and his family had suffered greatly, Clinton was unwilling to admit that his sin deserved any real consequence.

Confession must include a willingness to accept the penalty for sin. To do otherwise cheapens the grace that God offers and makes light of Christ's sacrifice. Ask God to show you your sin. Write your prayer for forgiveness below.

PRAYER
Heavenly Father, I know that the more I understand the seriousness of my sin, the better I will understand the magnificence of Your forgiveness. Amen.

_____

_____

_____

_____

COMING BACK TO GOD
Week 26: *Accept Consequences*
A SCAR TRANSFORMED Jonah 1:11–14

The sea was getting rougher and rougher. So they asked him, "What should we do to you to make the sea calm down for us?" "Pick me up and throw me into the sea," he replied, "and it will become calm. I know that it is my fault that this great storm has come upon you." Instead, the men did their best to row back to land. But they could not, for the sea grew even wilder than before. Then they cried out to the Lord, "Please, Lord, do not let us die for taking this man's life. Do not hold us accountable for killing an innocent man, for you, Lord, have done as you pleased."

Seven-year old Lucy wrote to God and asked, "Please make me better. I have a bad stomachache from too much candy again." (from *Dear Lord: Children's Letters to God* by Bill Adler) Lucy's prayer makes us smile. Her predicament is something we each know all too well.

Caught with our hand in the candy jar and feeling the pain of our actions, we run to God and ask Him to make it better. Though by now we should have learned our lesson, we give in again to an insatiable sin nature that won't quit until our bellies are sore.

Sin leaves a scar—a child neglects the aging parent who criticized rather than loved; a wife cannot trust again after her husband has an affair. But when transformed by God, the scars left by sin can be guideposts that keep us on a path close to Him and remind us of the limitless depth of His love.

What lasting reminder of sin do you bear? Reflect below on how God has used that reminder to your benefit.

PRAYER
Heavenly Father, help me to accept the consequences of my sin. Help me see Your discipline as a demonstration of Your amazing love. Amen.

COMING BACK TO GOD
Week 26: *Accept Consequences*

SCARS OF AN OLD LIFE

Jonah 1:15–16

Then they took Jonah and threw him overboard, and the raging sea grew calm. At this the men greatly feared the LORD, and they offered a sacrifice to the LORD and made vows to him.

Mel Trotter was a desperate alcoholic intent on suicide by the tender age of twenty-seven. A rescue worker found Trotter on the street one night in the middle of a Chicago blizzard. Trotter's life changed dramatically when he gave his heart to Christ. The alcoholic in need of rescue became a rescuer of others as he dedicated his life to leading others to Christ.

Trotter was a new man, but his old life had left a scar. When Trotter returned to his vocation as a barber in order to pay off nagging debts, his shaking hands often drew blood from customers. The marriage damaged by neglect during his years of drunken binges finally dissolved—at the height of Trotter's ministry.

In Christ, we are new creations, but the scars left by sin are reminders of where we've been. With God's grace, old scars can serve as warning posts that keep us away from sin's pitfalls and teach us the depth of His love.

PRAYER
Heavenly Father, help me to delight in Your forgiveness, accept the consequences of my sin, and see both as evidence of Your love. Amen.

COMING BACK TO GOD
Week 26: *Accept Consequences*
A GOD IN OUR IMAGE? Jonah 1:3

But Jonah ran away from the LORD...he went aboard and sailed for Tarshish to flee from the LORD.

The high school freshman was angry. Though verbal and written reminders had been issued for more than a week, she failed to bring to class the one item for a group project that was her responsibility to bring. Her neglect resulted in a poor grade. She stomped her foot at the teacher and said, "You mean you're holding me responsible for not bringing what I said I'd bring?"

In a society consumed with feeling good about itself, sin is a foreign concept. Immorality is excused with the presumption that if we're not concerned about sin, God won't be either. "The idea that retribution [making wrongs right] might be the moral law of God's world and an expression of his holy character seems to us quite fantastic," wrote J. I. Packer in *Knowing God*. Instead, Packer wrote that we've made God into an image of ourselves.

God's goodness requires that sin be accounted for. Below, confess whatever God reveals to you. When you're finished, write "paid in full."

PRAYER
Heavenly Father, help me understand that it is Your love and mercy that calls to me account for my sin. I love You. Amen.

Week 27: *Repent and Move Forward*
THE PRICE OF FREEDOM   John 3:16; John 8:1–2

For God so loved the world that he gave his one and only Son, that whoever believes in him shall not perish but have eternal life. *John 3:16*

But Jesus went to the Mount of Olives. At dawn he appeared again in the temple courts, where all the people gathered around him, and he sat down to teach them. *John 8:1–2*

At eleven weeks old, my daughter was very ill. The medical test at the Children's Hospital required that she be placed on a cold, stainless steel table, without the comfort of clothes. While activity buzzed around her, she locked her eyes on mine, and screamed. Not once did she look anywhere else. Tears streamed down my face, too, as I longed desperately to snatch her up in my arms and comfort her.

How God the Father must have suffered as Jesus, His only Son, hung on the cross. What an astonishing price was paid for salvation. Alister McGrath wrote, "The price of our freedom was the death of his one and only son. How much we must matter to this God if the price which is paid to redeem us is so great!" (*The Unknown God,* p. 87)

Are you amazed by what God has done? Below, reflect on how much you mean to God for Him to have paid so handsomely to redeem you.

PRAYER
Heavenly Father, forgive me for not taking sin and Your forgiveness as seriously as You do. Thank You for loving me. Amen.

_____

_____

_____

_____

_____

COMING BACK TO GOD
Week 27: *Repent and Move Forward*

THE SHEPHERD WHO SEEKS

John 3:17;
John 8:3–6a

For God did not send his Son into the world to condemn the world, but to save the world through him. *John 3:17*

The teachers of the law and the Pharisees brought in a woman caught in adultery. They made her stand before the group and said to Jesus, "Teacher, this woman was caught in the act of adultery. In the Law Moses commanded us to stone such women. Now what do you say?" They were using this question as a trap, in order to have a basis for accusing him. *John 8:3-6a*

One of the great themes of Scripture is that God seeks after the sinner. From the moment sin entered world through the Garden of Eden, God was on the move, searching out the law-breakers in order to rescue and restore.

"God chose to come to where we are. Instead of expecting us to find him, he comes to us," wrote Oxford theologian Alister McGrath in *The Unknown God* (p. 58). Like the shepherd in the parable of the lost sheep, Jesus came to us, found us, and gathered us in His arms to carry us back home. Because God seeks us, we can be confident of His love. Because Christ won forgiveness for us on the cross, we can live in freedom knowing our debt has been cancelled.

Reflect on what it means to say your sin is completely forgiven. Also reflect on what your salvation cost God. Make a commitment in the space below to live a life that honors Him. Record your reflections below.

PRAYER

Heavenly Father, thank You for finding me and saving me. Help me remember Your amazing and gracious love. Amen.

COMING BACK TO GOD
Week 27: *Repent and Move Forward*
UNSHACKLED — John 5:14–15; John 8:6b–8

Later Jesus found him at the temple and said to him, "See, you are well again. Stop sinning or something worse may happen to you." The man went away and told the Jewish leaders that it was Jesus who had made him well. *John 5:14–15*

But Jesus bent down and started to write on the ground with his finger. When they kept on questioning him, he straightened up and said to them, "Let any one of you who is without sin be the first to throw a stone at her." Again he stooped down and wrote on the ground.
John 8:6b–8

"I am a great sinner. Christ is a great Savior." These words of John Newton, the former slave trader whose life was radically changed by Christ, came alive in the film *Amazing Grace*. Newton's passion for the Gospel was driven by a deep sense of his sin and an inexpressible gratitude for the forgiveness he experienced in Christ.

Today's world doesn't understand grace because it doesn't understand sin. Our culture is crippled by the spirit of the age that says that critiquing another's actions or beliefs is paramount to hate. When critique is silenced, rescue efforts are impaired. Those who carry deep hurt or unhappiness remain shackled in hurtful behavior because society looks the other way. They need the good news that Christ forgives and breaks the power of sin.

List below the name of a friend or family member God places on your heart. Ask God to show you how to genuinely love them while showing them the way to freedom in Christ.

PRAYER
Heavenly Father, help me remember that my sin is covered by Your grace alone. Help me to share that message of hope with others. Amen.

COMING BACK TO GOD
Week 27: *Repent and Move Forward*
A FAILED TREATMENT John 3:19; John 8:9

This is the verdict: Light has come into the world, but people loved darkness instead of light because their deeds were evil. *John 3:19*

At this, those who heard began to go away one at a time, the older ones first, until only Jesus was left, with the woman still standing there. *John 8:9*

For months after the stock market crash of October 1929 that sent the nation into a decade-long depression, government officials continued to paint a rosy picture of the situation. Even as banks failed and long bread lines formed, President Herbert Hoover and administrators insisted all was okay. Historian Frederick Lewis Allen recorded, "The grim farce went on, the physicians uttering soothing words to the patient and the patient daily sinking lower and lower...Only when the failure of the treatment became obvious to the point of humiliation did the Administration lapse into temporary silence" (*Only Yesterday*, p. 259).

Our nation is sinking lower and lower into sin while the cultural physicians—the media, political pundits—refuse to acknowledge the severity of the disease. The world's treatment has failed. Only when we acknowledge our sin can we move forward into freedom, hope and deeply satisfying joy.

List below a problem or issue someone you love is facing. Pray as you write out a response to that issue that will communicate God's grace and forgiveness.

PRAYER
Heavenly Father, help me to communicate to others that Your forgiveness is liberating. Help me to truly love others. Amen.

COMING BACK TO GOD
Week 27: *Repent and Move Forward*

FORGIVEN! John 8:10–11

Jesus straightened up and asked her, "Woman, where are they? Has no one condemned you?" "No one, sir," she said. "Then neither do I condemn you," Jesus declared. "Go now and leave your life of sin."

Drugs and alcohol had been a part of B. J.'s life until he came to know Christ. All of that was put aside as he grew in the Lord. One day, B. J. pulled open his shirt to show the pastor his new tattoo. On his chest was this simple but bold statement: "God Forgave Me."

B. J. has remained faithful to the Lord in the years since that day and has raised his young family in the church. In many ways, his tattoo captures the heart of the Gospel. Faith should leave its mark on our lives, a radical change brought about because of the forgiveness of sins. Gratitude for God's forgiveness calls us to leave behind a life of sin. The true believer understands that salvation cannot be earned by a life of good deeds, but lives a life of service to others out of gratitude for what God has done.

Is the sense of forgiveness fresh in your life? Below, consider how your daily life would change if that sense of forgiveness was again fresh and new.

PRAYER
Heavenly Father, show me the sin that I need to confess. Let my life be a testimony to others of Your grace and forgiveness. Amen.

COMING BACK TO GOD
Week 28: *Find Restoration*

TODAY'S LESSON: FAILURE   Hebrews 9:6-12

When everything had been arranged like this, the priests entered regularly into the outer room to carry on their ministry. But only the high priest entered the inner room, and that only once a year, and never without blood, which he offered for himself and for the sins the people had committed in ignorance. The Holy Spirit was showing by this that the way into the Most Holy Place had not yet been disclosed as long as the first tabernacle was still functioning. This is an illustration for the present time, indicating that the gifts and sacrifices being offered were not able to clear the conscience of the worshiper. They are only a matter of food and drink and various ceremonial washings—external regulations applying until the time of the new order. But when Christ came as high priest of the good things that are now already here, he went through the greater and more perfect tabernacle that is not made with human hands, that is to say, is not a part of this creation. He did not enter by means of the blood of goats and calves; but he entered the Most Holy Place once for all by his own blood, thus obtaining eternal redemption.

Christians fail. We don't live up to Christ's example of love and grace nor do we follow His teachings for truthful, moral lives as we should. Our salvation is secure, yet our behavior can be anything but consistent. Is there any hope?

In *Mere Christianity*, C. S. Lewis wrote that believers, when they falter, should ask for forgiveness, pick themselves up, and "try again." This process of falling and coming back to God for forgiveness is not only inevitable, it is important. Lewis wrote, "We learn, on the one hand, that we cannot trust ourselves even in our best moments, and, on the other hand, that we need not despair even in our worst, for our failures are forgiven" (*Mere Christianity,* Book III, paragraph 12).

Christians must battle personal sin because we represent Christ to the world, yet our sin-weary world is hungry for our message of forgiveness and restoration. Use the space below to reflect on who might be blessed by your story of forgiveness and salvation.

PRAYER
Heavenly Father, help me to live in confidence knowing my sins are forgiven. Use my failures as a means to lead someone else to You. Amen.

COMING BACK TO GOD
Week 28: *Find Restoration*
KICKED TO THE CURB   Hebrews 9:13, 10:12–13

The blood of goats and bulls and the ashes of a heifer sprinkled on those who are ceremonially unclean sanctify them so that they are outwardly clean. *Hebrews 9:13*

But when this priest had offered for all time one sacrifice for sins, he sat down at the right hand of God, and since that time he waits for his enemies to be made his footstool. *Hebrews 10:12-13*

There were no chairs in the tabernacle or temple. A note in *The Student Bible* by Zondervan Publishing House (1996) on this passage states that Jewish priests didn't sit while performing their priestly duties. By standing, the priests symbolized that their work in offering sacrifices for the people's sin was never done. Yet, Jesus, our High Priest, "sat down" when His work on the Cross was finished. With Jesus' resurrection, a new covenant was instituted; the old was replaced with the new; the sacrifice for sin was complete.

Newness of life is a great theme of Scripture. Paul wrote to the believers in Corinth that when a person comes to Christ, he is "a new creation" (2 Corinthians 5:17). The past is over. The guilt and pain we once bore for sin can be kicked to the curb. Joy in abundance can be ours.

List below the things that trip you up in your walk with Christ. Ask God to give you victory over them.

PRAYER
Heavenly Father, I know Your Son paid for my sin. Help me to live in a way that is joyful and honors You. Amen.

COMING BACK TO GOD
Week 28: *Find Restoration*
FINISHED
Hebrews 10:14

For by one sacrifice he has made perfect forever those who are being made holy.

Sometimes people ask, "If God loves me, why doesn't He just forgive me? Why did Jesus have to die?" D. A. Carson answered this in *The God Who is There* when he wrote that while God wants to forgive, He "cannot pretend sin is not there...God's desire to forgive is paired with his insistence that sin be punished."

The unbeliever could be asked in turn, "Why don't you just forgive the person who slandered your name and stole your reputation? Or who lied to you?" When injustice becomes personal, we understand why wrong deeds must be punished.

In the Old Testament, sacrifices for sin were repeated each year: no offering could truly cover sin. Carson wrote: "The old Day of Atonement...has been superseded, because we have the ultimate sacrifice for sin: Jesus himself ...offers up his life, takes our death, and bears our sin away in a fashion that no animal ever could" (pp. 69-70).

For the believer, sin has been paid for. Reflect on this below, remembering that because of Christ, you are blameless and have no reason to feel shame.

PRAYER
Heavenly Father, help me remember that because my sin is forgiven in Christ, I can live joyfully. Amen.

COMING BACK TO GOD
Week 28: *Find Restoration*
NONE LIKE HIM
Hebrews 10:15–16; Micah 7:18

The Holy Spirit also testifies to us about this. First he says: "This is the covenant I will make with them after that time, says the Lord. I will put my laws in their hearts, and I will write them on their minds."
Hebrews 10:15–16

Who is a God like you, who pardons sin and forgives the transgression of the remnant of his inheritance? You do not stay angry forever but delight to show mercy. *Micah 7:18*

A humpback whale off the coast of Baja, California, was caught in a nylon net and suffered terribly. The crew on the boat who found her knew there was great risk in trying to help a forty-ton animal in pain. They deliberated, and then decided to help.

Partially untangled, the whale swam alongside the boat as the crew continued working for an hour to finish the job. Once freed, the whale lept for joy, making more than forty leaps into the air in a spectacular acrobatic display. The whale's reaction was called a "magnificent thank you" to the crew.

What a beautiful picture of forgiveness. With no thought of the nylon net and the bad decisions that had led to her being caught in a death-trap, the whale rejoiced. Past sin is removed. Christ has set us free.

Below, express your thankfulness to God, remembering the past is forgotten. Be sure to thank Him for what He's doing in your life right now.

PRAYER
Heavenly Father, thank You for freedom from every hurt I've caused and every pain I've experienced. Let my life be a testimony to Your forgiveness. Amen.

COMING BACK TO GOD
Week 28: *Find Restoration*

REMEMBERED NO MORE — Hebrews 10:17-18

Then he adds: "Their sins and lawless acts I will remember no more." And where these have been forgiven, sacrifice for sin is no longer necessary.

David Jeremiah in his book *Searching for Heaven on Earth* wrote that sometimes we dwell too long on the past as we lament the "good old days." Yesterday was better, less stressful, less troublesome, we think. But an idyllic past is a figment of the imagination. It too, was a mix of good things and bad.

In the same sense, we can think too long on sin. Dwelling on a past failure can paralyze a believer with self-doubt and guilt. God cannot bless me or use me, we insist, and we find ourselves unable to rise above fear and insecurity. Jeremiah wrote, "Meanwhile, the ultimate reality in life is God, who wants to fill your life with His presence and power right here and right now" (p. 189).

Scripture invites the believer to repent and move forward. Restoration is promised; help in overcoming the sin that continues to trip us up is available. In the space below, write the words of Hebrew 10:17 substituting your name for "their" and your list of failures for "their sins and lawless acts."

PRAYER
Heavenly Father, thank You for forgiving, and forgetting, my sin. Help me to move forward, confident of Your forgiveness. Amen.

COMING BACK TO GOD
Week 29: *Reconcile with Others*
A COMPELLED BY CHRIST Luke 3:8, 19:1–4

Produce fruit in keeping with repentance. *Luke 3:8*

Jesus entered Jericho and was passing through. A man was there by the name of Zacchaeus; he was a chief tax collector and was wealthy. He wanted to see who Jesus was, but because he was short he could not see over the crowd. So he ran ahead and climbed a sycamore-fig tree to see him, since Jesus was coming that way. *Luke 19:1–4*

In the classic novel *Les Miserables*, the convict Jean Valjean discovers grace when a humble priest refuses to charge him with thievery. Valjean begins a new life under an assumed name but is pursued by Javert, a police officer intent on finding him. When mistaken identity results in the arrest of the wrong man, Valjean is caught in a dilemma. The old Valjean would not have cared if someone paid for his crime; the new Valjean feels remorse. He wrestles bitterly with his conscience but, in the end, reveals himself as the real Valjean. The decision costs him dearly.

Grace should impact our lives and change our behavior. Becoming a new creation in Christ (2 Corinthians 5:17) should mean a radical shift in our motives, intentions, and actions. While growing in Christ may require difficult soul searching at times or may come at a price, in the end, the joy and peace of Christ will be found.

Has your faith radically affected your life? Use the space below to consider the mercy God has shown you.

PRAYER
Heavenly Father, help me to show mercy to others as You have shown mercy to me. Let my life reflect Your love. Amen.

COMING BACK TO GOD
Week 29: *Reconcile with Others*

A COMPELLED BY CHRIST Luke 19:5-7

When Jesus reached the spot, he looked up and said to him, "Zacchaeus, come down immediately. I must stay at your house today." So he came down at once and welcomed him gladly. All the people saw this and began to mutter, "He has gone to be the guest of a sinner."

Albert H. Quie, former president of Prison Fellowship Ministries, once told of meeting a stylishly dressed woman at a ministry banquet in Seattle. Her words astounded him: "The man I ate dinner with tonight killed my brother."

Ruth Youngsman told Quie she had met her brother's murderer twenty years after the crime as he worked on a dairy farm following his release from prison. She felt "compelled by Christ's command to forgive," Quie wrote in *Jubilee*, a publication of Prison Fellowship Ministries. Though the man was not a Christian, Youngsman became his friend, even to the point of bringing him to her father's side as he lay dying.

Offering forgiveness for such a heinous crime is an action the world does not understand. This kind of forgiveness can only happen when a person understands the extraordinary love of God.

Are there people you would consider unwelcome in your home? Do you overlook people who seem to be in circumstances of their own making? Reflect below.

PRAYER
Heavenly Father, help me to look past the circumstances and choices of others and see them as people whom You love. Amen.

COMING BACK TO GOD
Week 29: *Reconcile with Others*
CHANGE ME Luke 19:8

But Zacchaeus stood up and said to the Lord, "Look, Lord! Here and now I give half of my possessions to the poor, and if I have cheated anybody out of anything, I will pay back four times the amount."

Years ago, a town in Southeastern Louisiana had a general store called *The Leader* that was run by two sisters who didn't get along. They "split" the store down the middle with merchandise and cash registers on each side. Customers were made to pay for an item on the side of the store where it was picked up. Disagreement had led to a partnership that was in name only.

Relationships are fragile and when they break, the wound can fester and ooze. A thoughtless reply, a self-centered action, and a small disagreement can become an insurmountable wall of separation. Christ calls His followers to set right not only past monetary obligations, as Zachaeus did, but damaged relationships, as well.

Is there a relationship in your life that isn't what it should be? Write the name of the person below and commit to pray for him or her for a week.

PRAYER
Heavenly Father, change me in whatever way You see fit in order to make this relationship right. Help me to love the other person. Amen.

COMING BACK TO GOD
Week 29: *Reconcile with Others*

MENDING WHAT'S BROKEN   Luke 19:9–10

Jesus said to him, "Today salvation has come to this house, because this man, too, is a son of Abraham. For the Son of Man came to seek and to save the lost."

The story is told of a husband and wife who became estranged, then finally separated with each moving to a different part of the country. One day, the husband returned on business to the city where they once lived. While there, he decided to visit the grave of the couple's only son. He stood at the grave remembering better times when he heard a step behind him. It was his wife.

The couple's first inclination was to turn away from each other again, but something stopped them. The one bond between them, the one interest they still shared, was their son. Standing over his grave hand-in-hand became a first step toward reconciliation. It took the death of their son to bring them back together.

The death of God's Son reconciled humanity to God. Because we are made new people in Christ, the mending of broken relationships is possible. Reflect below on what it means for your life to be reconciled to God.

PRAYER
Heavenly Father, thank You that You came looking for me. Help me show Your love to others. Amen.

COMING BACK TO GOD
Week 29: *Reconcile with Others*
SETTING WRONGS RIGHT
Matthew 5:23–24

Therefore, if you are offering your gift at the altar and there remember that your brother or sister has something against you, leave your gift there in front of the altar. First go and be reconciled to them; then come and offer your gift.

President George W. Bush once referred to American slavery as "one of the greatest crimes of history." He added that "many of the issues that still trouble America have roots in the bitter experience of other times."

For the Southern Baptist Convention, the past was something delegates of the 150th convention wanted to set right. A resolution passed that year acknowledged that slavery played a role when the convention formed in the mid-nineteenth century. The act apologized for "condoning and/or perpetuating individual and systemic racism in our lifetime" and made a commitment to eradicate racism throughout Southern Baptist life. Seventeen years later, the Reverend Fred Luter, Jr., a New Orleans pastor, was elected president, the first African-American to hold the position.

True repentance requires that wrongs be made right. As believers, we are required to make the first steps toward reconciliation. Use the space below to consider the impact reconciliation would have in your relationships; in your church; in our nation.

PRAYER
Heavenly Father, show me what I need to do to mend broken relationships. Make me Your ambassador for grace and reconciliation. Amen.

COMING BACK TO GOD
Week 30: *Represent God Anew*
I'M GOING THAT WAY   1 Timothy 1:12

I thank Christ Jesus our Lord, who has given me strength, that he considered me trustworthy, appointing me to his service.

Just north of Hillsboro, Texas, Interstate 35 splits. One branch, 35W, turns northwest and runs through Fort Worth; the other, 35E, goes through Dallas. Travelers frequently get lost when they confuse the two main arteries that feed the sixty-mile wide metroplex.

At a stop along the interstate one day, a man frantic for directions approached my husband. The man needed to find a particular funeral home in a hurry—the hearse he was driving had the deceased inside. My husband tried to explain the way back, but to no avail. Finally he said, "Just follow me. I'm going that way." Twenty minutes later, a much relieved hearse driver was on the right road.

It's easy to tell others what to do, but when we love others enough to walk beside them, we can make a lasting difference. We can show the way to Christ. Make a list of the places you've been this week. Reflect on how God has used you, or could have used you, to share His love in each place.

PRAYER
Heavenly Father, help me to share Your love by investing my life in others. Amen.

COMING BACK TO GOD
Week 30: *Represent God Anew*
EVERY DAY AND EVERYWHERE 1 Timothy 1:13; Psalm 71:15

Even though I was once a blasphemer and a persecutor and a violent man, I was shown mercy because I acted in ignorance and unbelief.
1 Timothy 1:13

My mouth will tell of your righteous deeds, of your saving acts all day long—though I know not how to relate them all. Psalm 71:15

A retired insurance salesman once explained to me why he "pestered" people about insurance. Years ago, a client lost a young son. The family's horrific loss was compounded by financial devastation from medical bills and the cost of the funeral. "As their agent, I felt responsible because they didn't have the coverage they needed," he said. "From then on, I made it a point to talk to everybody I knew and everybody I met about insurance." The incident changed his life. Even when people avoided him or tried to change the subject, he continued talking about insurance at every turn.

Sadly, the man was not a Christian and didn't want to talk about the Gospel. After he shared this story, I said, "That is exactly how Christians feel. We talk about Christ every chance we get because it's so important."

Are you willing to talk about Christ even when others don't want to hear? In light of this story, write out a response or a question you might have asked my friend in that situation.

PRAYER
Heavenly Father, help me to feel the urgency of sharing the Gospel with others. Give me courage to do so. Amen.

COMING BACK TO GOD
Week 30: *Represent God Anew*
CHANGED BY LOVE 1 Timothy 1:14; 2 Corinthians 1:3-4

The grace of our Lord was poured out on me abundantly, along with the faith and love that are in Christ Jesus. *1 Timothy 1:14*

Praise be to...the Father of compassion and the God of all comfort, who comforts us in all our troubles, so that we can comfort those in any trouble with the comfort we ourselves receive from God.
2 Corinthians 1:3-4

Mary Ann Bird was born with a cleft palate. The result was misshapen lips, lopsided teeth, and garbled speech. When children asked what happened to her lip, she would say, "I cut it on a piece of glass." In her memoir, *The Whisper Test,* she wrote: "Somehow it seemed more acceptable to have suffered an accident than to have been born different. I was convinced that nobody outside my family could love me."

Then, Mary Ann met Mrs. Leonard. Each year the popular teacher tested her students' hearing by whispering in an ear something like "the sky is blue" or "Do you have a dog?" that the child would repeat. When Mary Ann's turn came, Mrs. Leonard whispered, "I wish you were my little girl." Later, Mary Ann wrote that "God must have put into her mouth those seven words that changed my life."

Whose life could you change by showing Christ-like compassion? Write out below encouraging words that you can say to someone in need.

PRAYER
Heavenly Father, help me show genuine compassion to those I meet. Let me love as You do. Amen.

COMING BACK TO GOD
Week 30: *Represent God Anew*

RESCUED!   1 Timothy 1:15

Here is a trustworthy saying that deserves full acceptance: Christ Jesus came into the world to save sinners—of whom I am the worst.

The video of the rescue of a little girl in China caught the attention of the international news media recently. A man on his way to work scaled a three-story apartment building when he saw it was on fire. The child he rescued was trapped in her family's apartment, locked inside for her safety by parents who had to leave for work.

The world's imagination was captured not only by the man's diligence in scaling the tall building, but by the fact that he climbed it twice: once to see if anyone was inside, and a second time carrying the axe and ropes he needed to bring the little girl to safety.

Like Paul before his conversion, many people are trapped in beliefs that are sincere, yet futile. Good intentions, like those of the parents in this story, do not save. We need a Rescuer. Are you willing to do the extraordinary to lead someone to Christ? Commit below to let God use you in a new and fresh way.

PRAYER
Heavenly Father, thank You for saving me. Give me the resources and courage I need to share Christ with others. Amen.

COMING BACK TO GOD
Week 30: *Represent God Anew*
JUST AS I AM   1 Timothy 1:16–17

But for that very reason I was shown mercy so that in me, the worst of sinners, Christ Jesus might display his immense patience as an example for those who would believe in him and receive eternal life. Now to the King eternal, immortal, invisible, the only God, be honor and glory for ever and ever. Amen.

Charlotte Elliott was an invalid from her youth and deeply resented God. One day, her bitterness spilled over to a visiting preacher. The cure to her bitterness was the God she despised, he told her. When she asked how to find peace and joy, he answered, "Give yourself to God just as you are now, with your fightings and fears, hates and loves, pride and shame."

That day, Charlotte Elliott came to faith in Christ. Years later, she penned the now-famous hymn *Just As I Am*. Though she battled ill health and thoughts of self-condemnation throughout life, her words have helped countless others find Christ. She wrote: "Just as I am, though tossed about, With many a conflict, many a doubt, fightings within, and fears without, O Lamb of God, I come."

God will use whatever you commit to Him. Below, list any struggle, trial, gift or blessing you have in life. Then, commit them all to God.

PRAYER
Heavenly Father, I give You every heartache and every blessing. Thank you for loving me. Use me as You wish. Amen.

RELATING TO OTHERS
Week 31: *Made for Each Other*

NOT ALONE
Genesis 2:18

The LORD God said, "It is not good for the man to be alone. I will make a helper suitable for him."

In the movie *The Wizard of Oz,* Dorothy keeps trying to find someone to send her home. In the end, she's told that she always had the ability to get home, but that she had to learn that for herself. What she had learned was to recognize the things that were most important to her.

God created man to live in relationship with Him. But, He also created man to be in relationship with others. That can be seen in the order of God's creation. Notice that in verse 18, God stated man's need to be in relationship with another, but in verses 19-20, God brought all the creatures He had created before man to be named. In the process of identifying every living creature, man realized that there was no other creature like him. It was only in that process of discovery that man was able to recognize that most basic need.

What have you learned about yourself and relationships through your personal experiences? How have these lessons taught you about God? What does it mean to you to be created for relationship with God and with others? Respond below.

PRAYER
Heavenly Father, You created me and You know me. Help me recognize how to live in relationship...both with You and with others. Amen.

_____

_____

_____

_____

_____

RELATING TO OTHERS
Week 31: *Made for Each Other*
SUITABLE HELPER Genesis 2:19–20

Now the Lord God had formed out of the ground all the wild animals and all the birds in the sky. He brought them to the man to see what he would name them; and whatever the man called each living creature, that was its name. So the man gave names to all the livestock, the birds in the sky and all the wild animals. But for Adam no suitable helper was found.

One of the joys we've experienced while working with senior adults is witnessing what life-long, Christian relationships look like. It's not unusual to watch a couple celebrate their 60th wedding anniversary and some have been together much longer than that. These couples are a testimony of what it means to find someone to be a "suitable helper" with whom to share life.

In today's society, the phrase "suitable helper" is not always valued. We live in a culture that encourages independence, self-expression, and success. Often, those who receive the most attention are those who are working the hardest to prove themselves before others. But, God's desire was to create a relationship that mirrored His relationship with man...one that was based on love, respect, and mutual support.

Below, respond to these questions: Have you considered what makes another person "suitable" in a relationship with you? What does that mean to you? How is your relationship with God reflected in the relationships you have with others?

PRAYER
Father God, teach me what it means to be in holy relationship—with You and with others. Amen.

RELATING TO OTHERS
Week 31: *Made for Each Other*

DEEP SLEEP
Genesis 2:21-22

So the LORD God caused the man to fall into a deep sleep; and while he was sleeping, he took one of the man's ribs and then closed up the place with flesh. Then the LORD God made a woman from the rib he had taken out of the man, and he brought her to the man.

As a fifteen-year-old Boy Scout, I was tapped out to become part of the Order of the Arrow. I was blindfolded, taken out into the words, and left alone to spend the night. I slept so deeply that night that another selected scout had to kick me awake before we could find our way back to camp. Being put in that situation was designed to allow me to prove I had the skills to get back on my own. But the night in the woods represented a significant rite of passage in my life.

God put the first man into a deep sleep—a divinely given sleep—that was also a rite of passage. While the man slept, God personally created woman as a "suitable helper" to join him. She was like the man and yet different than him. She was specifically created to complement the man. Together in relationship, they could be better than they would have been alone. What a God-given gift they both received.

Think about what it means to know that God created both man and woman to be both distinct and complementary to each other. How does that difference demonstrate God's love for all mankind? Respond below.

PRAYER
Heavenly Father, thank You for knowing what I need in my life. Help me find relationships that reflect the care You have shown me. Amen.

RELATING TO OTHERS
Week 31: *Made for Each Other*

BECOMING ONE FLESH — Genesis 2:23–24

The man said, "This is now bone of my bones and flesh of my flesh; she shall be called 'woman,' for she was taken out of man." That is why a man leaves his father and mother and is united to his wife, and they become one flesh.

My wife had major surgery recently. It's been difficult watching her experience the pain of recovery as her body knits itself back together. I can remember early days in our marriage when we also experienced the growing pains of our new relationship. Having a successful marriage takes work.

In a seminary class I took many years ago, I heard a lecture of what it meant to become "one flesh." The professor emphasized that becoming "one flesh" is more than just having a sexual relationship, but is a coming together of the minds, the emotions, and the very lives of man and wife. He suggested that many marriages end long before the process of becoming one flesh ever happens because the process takes time and work.

These verses indicate what a godly marriage is like. It's built on becoming a new unit, apart from all other relationships, which approaches life as one. Consider the following questions and then respond to the final question below: What Godly marriages have you witnessed? How did these marriages demonstrate this Biblical picture of marriage? If you are married, what do you want your marriage to be like?

PRAYER
Heavenly Father, thank You for the gift of marriage. Help me to support those who are struggling to have a godly marriage. Teach me to love another as You have loved us. Amen.

RELATING TO OTHERS
Week 31: *Made for Each Other*

NO SHAME
Genesis 2:25

Adam and his wife were both naked, and they felt no shame.

One of the earliest emotions a child learns to express, after joy, is shame. Catch a child in the act of doing something wrong, and the child will deny he or she did anything wrong. When our children were around two and denying their guilt, it was kind of funny. Shame, however, comes from recognizing sin that needs to be confessed. There's nothing funny about it.

In verse 25, the Hebrew word that is translated "naked" refers to being without clothes. But the Hebrew word translated "naked" in Genesis 3:7, after Adam and woman had sinned, is the same word used in Deuteronomy 28:48 and includes being found guilty before God. Scholars suggest that after sin, Adam and his wife understood what it meant to be found guilty before God.

Adam and Eve were created to live in relationship in a way that glorified God. Yet their sin caused them to experience the shame of disobedience before Holy God. How do you feel when standing before God? Do you feel the shame of disobedience and failure? Record your feelings below and then ask God to help you deal with the sin and shame in your life.

PRAYER
Father, You know what it means to be sinless and yet You love me in spite of my sin. Help me be willing to confess the sin in my life before You. Amen.

RELATING TO OTHERS
Week 32: *Love One Another*

REMAIN IN LOVE John 15:9–10

As the Father has loved me, so have I loved you. Now remain in my love. If you keep my commands, you will remain in my love, just as I have kept my Father's commands and remain in his love.

The long married couple was stopped at a traffic light when the wife noticed the young couple in the car next to them sitting as close to each other as humanly possible. "Why don't we ever sit like that," she asked from her spot next to the passenger side window. "I don't know," her husband replied. "I'm sitting in the same spot I've always been in. You're the one that moved." I love that story. Change in a relationship happens when one of the members moves away.

When Jesus taught His disciples about His love for them, He reminded them to "remain" in that love. The King James translation uses the word *abide*. The word *remain* means to stay with or to stay behind with. The word *abide* adds more: to endure with yielding; to accept without objection; to remain in a stable condition. To remain in God's love is abiding in it... remaining in it, not moving away, and accepting all that comes with that love. When we have the Father's love, why would we ever want to move off to the side to be by ourselves?

Begin this week intentionally abiding in God's love. Sit in a chair looking out a window and think what it means to be abiding (remaining) in God's love. Then, step away from the chair and consider how you've possibly moved away from Him. Journal below your experience.

PRAYER
My Father, teach me to abide in You. Help me know how to remain in Your love. Amen.

RELATING TO OTHERS
Week 32: *Love One Another*
LOVE EACH OTHER John 15:11–12

I have told you this so that my joy may be in you and that your joy may be complete. My command is this: Love each other as I have loved you.

In part of a song that was written for the movie *The Sound of Music* (although this part was cut out), Oscar Hammerstein wrote: "Love in your heart wasn't put there to stay. Love isn't love 'til you give it away." I didn't know the source of the quote until I googled it. But I had learned the quote from a poster that hung on my soon-to-be wife's dorm room wall. To me, that quote has always seemed to capture the essence of the Christian faith.

Jesus reminded His disciples of what would happen when they remained in God's love—God's love would come full circle when they loved others with the love of God. Notice the use of the word "complete." Try drawing a circle and leave a part of the circle open. Is it a circle? No, it's an arc. The circle is only a circle when it is completed. And God's love in us is made complete only when we love others with the same love that He has shown us.

Below, record your understanding of how God loves you. Then, evaluate that statement on how well you demonstrate that love to others. Are you loving others just as God loves you?

PRAYER
Heavenly Father, thank You for loving me. Help me know how to love others just like You have loved me. Amen.

_____

_____

_____

_____

_____

RELATING TO OTHERS
Week 32: *Love One Another*
THE GREATEST LOVE John 15:13–14

Greater love has no one than this: to lay down one's life for one's friends. You are my friends if you do what I command.

My father-in-law served on the front lines in World War II. When another soldier received a severe head injury, Clayton picked up the soldier and carried him to the aid station for help. On the way, a lieutenant threatened Clayton with a court martial if he didn't leave the man to die and return to his post. Clayton responded, "You do what you have to do, sir, and I'll do what I have to do." Clayton's actions saved the other soldier's life. There was no court martial.

When we asked Clayton about his response to the lieutenant, he explained that as a Christian, there was no other option for him but to take care of the other soldier. For Clayton, his actions were an extension of his faith. Jesus described that kind of faith when He told His disciples that they were to put the lives of others before their own. Obviously, Jesus knew the cost of what He required as shortly afterwards, He allowed His life to be taken for us.

What is the greatest act of love you've witnessed? How does that act reflect Christ's act on the cross?

PRAYER
Jesus, You are My Lord and Savior. You gave Your life for me. Show me how to love You and love others the way You love me. Amen.

RELATING TO OTHERS
Week 32: *Love One Another*
FULLY VESTED IN THE WORK — John 15:15–16

I no longer call you servants, because a servant does not know his master's business. Instead, I have called you friends, for everything that I learned from my Father I have made known to you. You did not choose me, but I chose you and appointed you so that you might go and bear fruit—fruit that will last—and so that whatever you ask in my name the Father will give you.

In the law field, success is often recognized when an attorney is made a partner in the firm. Before partnership, the attorney was only a worker, doing what he was instructed without knowing everything about the company. With partnership, the attorney is included in all the inner workings and secrets of the firm. The attorney has become completely vested in the work.

Jesus described the change in His relationship with His disciples. They had been servants and followers as they learned about Him and about His God. But now, Jesus elevated them to become friends—even partners—in His ministry. They would no longer just do what He told them to do, but they would begin to take responsibility for the ministry. They would be fully vested in the work of leading others to Jesus.

What does it mean to be fully vested in God's work? Evaluate your life. Are you fully vested in His work? Why? What would need to change for you to be fully vested? Respond below.

PRAYER
Heavenly Father, thank You for Your confidence in me, for making me a part of Your work. Help me know how to do that. Amen.

RELATING TO OTHERS
Week 32: *Love One Another*
LOVE EACH OTHER John 15:17

This is my command: Love each other.

One of the dangers in ministry is trying so hard to do the right things—reach the community, build a building, enroll new members—that individuals and their needs can go unnoticed and unmet. Staff members are often evaluated by "nickels and noses"—that is, how much money is in the offering and how many people are present. The need to meet those expectations can keep staff members so busy that they have little time for taking care of those who are hurting in the congregation.

Jesus' words in verse 17 must be understood as the conclusion of verses 15–16. Jesus had encouraged His disciples to take responsibility for the ministry and to go out and produce fruit in the lives of those who did not know Him. But He also reminded them not to get so busy doing the right things for those outside the church that they stopped loving those inside the church. His love has to be shown inside the congregation just as much as to those outside.

Think about your congregation. How does your congregation show love to those outside your church? How does your congregation show love to those inside your church? How do you participate in both? What are the strengths and weaknesses of your congregation? In your own life? Respond below.

PRAYER
Heavenly Father, show us, show me, how to love You more. Show us, show me, how to love others more. Show me ways that I've not done all I can in loving those around me. Amen.

RELATING TO OTHERS
Week 33: *In Relationship*
FRIENDSHIP BASED ON TRUST 1 Samuel 20:1-4

Then David fled from Naioth at Ramah and went to Jonathan and asked, "What have I done? What is my crime? How have I wronged your father, that he is trying to kill me?" "Never!" Jonathan replied. "You are not going to die! Look, my father doesn't do anything, great or small, without letting me know. Why would he hide this from me? It isn't so!" But David took an oath and said, "Your father knows very well that I have found favor in your eyes, and he has said to himself, 'Jonathan must not know this or he will be grieved.' Yet as surely as the LORD lives and as you live, there is only a step between me and death." Jonathan said to David, "Whatever you want me to do, I'll do for you."

Few relationships are completely trustworthy. News stories abound of parents who have abused their children, and spouses who have betrayed their partners. It's not difficult to recognize how many friendships are destroyed when one friend betrays another. Unfortunately, even the church can become a fertile field for distrust and betrayal.

David was in the position that he couldn't trust anyone around him—not the king, the guards, or any one else in the palace—except for his friend Jonathan. That could have caused David difficulties, since Jonathan was the son of Saul, the one who wanted David dead. But David knew that he could completely trust Jonathan, even when it came to things that involved Jonathan's father. Although Jonathan had difficulty believing the worst about his father, he never broke trust with David. It is that mutual trust—a trust that was firmly planted in their relationship with God—that makes the relationship between David and Jonathan so noteworthy.

Who can you trust completely? How does your trust level impact your relationships? Are you trustworthy as well? Respond below.

PRAYER
Heavenly Father, teach me what it means to be trustworthy in my relationships with others. Help me recognize that characteristic in others. Amen.

171

RELATING TO OTHERS
Week 33: *In Relationship*
FRIENDSHIP BASED ON LOYALTY 1 Samuel 20:5-11

So David said, "Look, tomorrow is the New Moon feast, and I am supposed to dine with the king; but let me go and hide in the field until the evening of the day after tomorrow. If your father misses me at all, tell him, 'David earnestly asked my permission to hurry to Bethlehem, his hometown, because an annual sacrifice is being made there for his whole clan.' If he says, 'Very well,' then your servant is safe. But if he loses his temper, you can be sure that he is determined to harm me. As for you, show kindness to your servant, for you have brought him into a covenant with you before the LORD. If I am guilty, then kill me yourself! Why hand me over to your father?" "Never!" Jonathan said. "If I had the least inkling that my father was determined to harm you, wouldn't I tell you?" David asked, "Who will tell me if your father answers you harshly?" "Come," Jonathan said, "let's go out into the field." So they went there together.

Having divided loyalty is tough. It's not unusual to see car tags that proclaim a house divided by different allegiances to rival schools. In my wife's extended family, a Georgia–Tennessee football game can almost lead to fights. Luckily, as important as the outcome of the game is each year, it is not life changing.

Jonathan could have been really caught in a position of divided loyalty between his father and his friend. His father Saul was king and had all the power. He expected Jonathan's allegiance because of their family relationship. Up against Saul's power, David had nothing...except for the loyalty of Jonathan. He could expect Jonathan's loyalty because their relationship was based on a covenant rendered before God. Jonathan sided with the relationship that was holy before God. He remained loyal to David when David needed him the most.

Jesus told His hearers that all who believed would have to make tough choices of remaining loyal to family or to God (see Matthew 10:35–39). What divided loyalties do you have? Are they influenced by your faith? How?

PRAYER
My Father, remind me daily that my loyalty begins with You. Help me approach holy things with undivided loyalty and help me build relationships that are reflective of my loyalty to You. Amen.

RELATING TO OTHERS
Week 33: *In Relationship*
FRIENDSHIP BASED ON RESPECT 1 Samuel 20:12-15

Then Jonathan said to David, "I swear by the LORD, the God of Israel, that I will surely sound out my father by this time the day after tomorrow! If he is favorably disposed toward you, will I not send you word and let you know? But if my father intends to harm you, may the LORD deal with Jonathan, be it ever so severely, if I do not let you know and send you away in peace. May the LORD be with you as he has been with my father. But show me unfailing kindness like the LORD's kindness as long as I live, so that I may not be killed, and do not ever cut off your kindness from my family—not even when the LORD has cut off every one of David's enemies from the face of the earth."

Before I officiated at my daughter's wedding, I met with her and my soon to be son-in-law and talked about the importance on having their ceremony in church and before the people who had been significant in their lives. I reminded them of the people who would be there as witnesses—family, friends, and those who had been a part of their journeys in faith. I reminded them that it was a holy thing to make the covenant in which they would live before these witnesses. God's covenants are holy and demand to be respected by all those who enter into them.

David and Jonathan's relationship existed in a covenant relationship, one that had been forged before God and based on their understanding of God's covenant with His people. Look at the language in this passage: *May the LORD deal, show me unfailing kindness like the LORD's kindness, do not cut off your kindness from my family.* Reread the passage beginning with verse 8 and continue through verse 17 and notice how firmly their relationship is three-sided. It's between them and God. Their relationship is the very picture of a holy covenant.

Do you have a relationship (or relationships) that model this covenantal bond? What makes the relationship function this way for you? Is there anything you would change in the relationship? Respond below:

PRAYER
My Father, show me ways that my relationships fail to live up to Your expectations. Amen.

_____

_____

_____

RELATING TO OTHERS
Week 33: *In Relationship*
FRIENDSHIP BASED ON PROMISE 1 Samuel 20:16–17

So Jonathan made a covenant with the house of David, saying, "May the LORD call David's enemies to account." And Jonathan had David reaffirm his oath out of love for him, because he loved him as he loved himself.

Celebrities have made the news recently by renewing their wedding vows annually. Sadly, in spite of the renewed promises, some of those marriages have still failed. A renewal of a covenant requires a new commitment to everything the original covenant entailed. But a renewal indicates a continuation of that commitment. God demonstrated that type of commitment when He renewed His covenant with Abraham and Isaac and Jacob. God showed that the original covenant continued on through each of the patriarchs.

During this time of extreme uneasiness and danger for David, Jonathan renewed the covenant the two had made. The renewal demonstrated that, despite the change in David's circumstances and the possible threat to David and Jonathan's relationship, their covenant agreement had not changed. It is a beautiful picture of God's covenant as well. No matter what circumstances we've experienced, God's covenant with us has not changed. It is the one unbroken promise we'll ever truly experience.

Reflect on the promise of God's love in your life. How do you depend upon that promise? How does that promise impact your relationships with others? Respond below.

PRAYER
My Father, thank You for loving me so much that You've not only promised me eternal life but provided Your Son to pay the price of that for me. Help me live in that promise daily. Amen.

_____

_____

_____

_____

_____

RELATING TO OTHERS
Week 33: *In Relationship*
FRIENDSHIP IN GOD 1 Samuel 20:42

Jonathan said to David, "Go in peace, for we have sworn friendship with each other in the name of the Lord, saying, 'The Lord is witness between you and me, and between your descendants and my descendants forever.'" Then David left, and Jonathan went back to the town.

When times have been the toughest on us—death of a parent, my wife's surgery that left her unable to walk for two months—we've relied on two things to survive those times. The first is our absolute conviction that God is in charge and will not abandon us. The second is the loving support of our Christian community. In our worship service each week, we close by "passing of the peace" to each other. In times of difficulty, we've experienced the "passing of the peace" in action.

Read 1 Samuel 20:18–42 and notice how dark David's world had become. His life was threatened and his existence as he had known it was over. The one constant David could depend upon, however, was the relational covenant that he and Jonathan had made. In David's darkest hours, Jonathan reaffirmed that covenant again, giving David a promise that would help him through the tough times to come. David and Jonathan's relationship can help us see how we as Christians can demonstrate the friendship we have that is special because it reflects our relationship with God.

Think about how you have received support from your Christian community as you've experienced tough times. Also, think about how you have supported others as well. How has the experience of receiving that support impacted your understanding of God's love? Respond below.

PRAYER
My Father, thank You for Your love and for teaching me to love others. Thank You for allowing me to experience that love through others. Amen.

_____

_____

_____

_____

RELATING TO OTHERS
Week 34: *Relationships that Last*
LASTING RELATIONSHIPS 2 Samuel 9:1

David asked, "Is there anyone still left of the house of Saul to whom I can show kindness for Jonathan's sake?"

Extended family relationships can be remarkably enduring. After decades of no contact, my wife and her sister have reconnected with their dad's side of the family. They've renewed old friendships, and made new ones, with cousins and their children. The one thing that binds them together is their shared past.

After years of war, King Saul and Jonathan were dead and David had become king. It was standard procedure for a new king to remove any threat to his reign by removing (killing) any one who had a claim to his throne—in this case any remaining members of Saul's family. But David acted out of his covenant promise to Jonathan, and looked for anyone from that family he could show kindness to on Jonathan's behalf. Their covenant to each other continued even after death.

How have you seen relationships be eternal? What makes relationships last? How do these relationships mirror our relationship with God? Respond below.

PRAYER
Heavenly Father, let me live in confidence of my relationship with You, one that will last beyond all time. Help me learn to build that kind of relationship with others. Amen.

RELATING TO OTHERS
Week 34: *Relationships that Last*
INTENTIONAL ACTION
2 Samuel 9:2–5

Now there was a servant of Saul's household named Ziba. They summoned him to appear before David, and the king said to him, "Are you Ziba?" "At your service," he replied. The king asked, "Is there no one still alive from the house of Saul to whom I can show God's kindness?" Ziba answered the king, "There is still a son of Jonathan; he is lame in both feet." "Where is he?" the king asked. Ziba answered, "He is at the house of Makir son of Ammiel in Lo Debar." So King David had him brought from Lo Debar, from the house of Makir son of Ammiel.

Many of us are drowning in our good intentions. We intend to check on a friend, help out with an autistic child, or take food to a friend in need. Most people grieving from a death of someone close to them discover that, after about three months, the care and concern they have received seems to stop. Good intentions remain, but other things take precedence.

David had asked about who was left in Jonathan's family that he could show care to. He could have stopped there. His question indicated his good intentions. But, David did more—he acted on those intentions by taking the next step and actively searching for Jonathan's family members. Good intentions could have made him feel like he was doing the right thing. Acting on those intentions demonstrated the depth of his commitment to Jonathan. What David found was shocking...Jonathan's son was crippled and living in shame. He desperately needed David's help.

Do you fall victim to "good intentions" without follow-through? Do you take intentional actions to support those who are in relationship with you? Below, list the strengths and weaknesses you bring to relationships. Then, prayerfully consider how you can use these in your current relationships, even your relationship with God.

PRAYER
Heavenly Father, help me act on my good intentions. Help me recognize the need of those with whom I have relationships and give me the wisdom to know how to help meet that need. Amen.

RELATING TO OTHERS
Week 34: *Relationships that Last*
OLD EXPECTATIONS   2 Samuel 9:6–8

When Mephibosheth son of Jonathan, the son of Saul, came to David, he bowed down to pay him honor. David said, "Mephibosheth!" "At your service," he replied. "Don't be afraid," David said to him, "for I will surely show you kindness for the sake of your father Jonathan. I will restore to you all the land that belonged to your grandfather Saul, and you will always eat at my table." Mephibosheth bowed down and said, "What is your servant, that you should notice a dead dog like me?"

My wife has now had two surgeries on her right foot. During each recovery, she's struggled to do things that have been taken for granted, like climbing a couple of stairs. She's also struggled to learn to do things differently, like using crutches and depending upon other people. As the recovery process lengthened from weeks to months, she struggled to accept the challenges, to remain patient, and to continue to accept help from others. It was obviously a difficult process for her.

Jonathan's son Mephibosheth faced those struggles for most of his life. He had been dropped by a nanny at the age of five and suffered permanent deformities in both feet. Any kind of physical deformity brought shame upon the bearer, so Mephibosheth was living his life out in exile. When David sent for him, he must have been frightened and expecting to be punished for his family background. Look at how he described himself—"a dead dog like me." Mephibosheth expected nothing good and could only envision the worst happening.

We don't like to dwell on the bad times in our lives, but often those can create for us expectations of more pain, more humiliation, even more shame. The action of Christ upon the cross removes all the pain, the humiliation, and the shame of our past, and brings us as healed people before God. How has Christ removed your pain and healed your sorrows?

PRAYER
Heavenly Father, thank You for not allowing me to live my entire life in pain and humiliation and suffering. Thank You for Your love through Your Son's actions to make me whole. Amen.

_____

_____

_____

RELATING TO OTHERS
Week 34: *Relationships that Last*

NEW PROMISES
2 Samuel 9:9–11a

Then the king summoned Ziba, Saul's steward, and said to him, "I have given your master's grandson everything that belonged to Saul and his family. You and your sons and your servants are to farm the land for him and bring in the crops, so that your master's grandson may be provided for. And Mephibosheth, grandson of your master, will always eat at my table." (Now Ziba had fifteen sons and twenty servants.) Then Ziba said to the king, "Your servant will do whatever my lord the king commands his servant to do."

Our senior adults have partnered with Street Grace, a ministry in our area that brings hope to women who have been involved in human trafficking. Most of these women feel deformed and worthless and see no options for their futures. Our senior adults, having experienced God's grace throughout their lives, desire to pass that onto these women. They desire to share God's promise of the future with those who can't see beyond their pasts.

David established a new covenant with Mephibosheth, and promised to give Mephibosheth everything that had once belonged to King Saul. Notice the difference in this covenant from the covenant between David and Jonathan. David and Jonathan made a reciprocal agreement and promised care for each other. However, David asked nothing from Mephibosheth but that he accept David's favor. Not only would Mephibosheth be taken care of, he would have a permanent place at the king's table. David's promises were life changing. Is there a better picture of grace except for the grace of God?

Describe God's grace in your life below. How have you been restored through His grace? How have you seen God's grace restore your relationships?

PRAYER
Heavenly Father, thank You for restoring me to be the person You know I can be. Help me live up to that promise. And help me use that promise to strengthen my relationships. Amen.

RELATING TO OTHERS
Week 34: *Relationships that Last*
SHARING THE TABLE   2 Samuel 9:11b–13

So Mephibosheth ate at David's table like one of the king's sons. Mephibosheth had a young son named Mika, and all the members of Ziba's household were servants of Mephibosheth. And Mephibosheth lived in Jerusalem, because he always ate at the king's table; he was lame in both feet.

At my in-laws' house, family dinners have become a spectacular picture of what God's table looks like. Thirty to forty people will gather and include four generations from two different families, plus some of the extended families from those generations, and friends of some of the younger members. To round out the table, some people are there because they have no family locally or no place to go. The one common element is the faith connection that binds us all into one huge family.

David made Mephibosheth one of his family. In spite of his perceived physical short-comings, David saw Mephibosheth as the valued son of his friend and treated him as such. The apostle Paul wrote that we have become heirs with Christ to God's Kingdom (Colossians 3:24). We have been given a place at His table. David's actions for Mephibosheth gives us a glimpse of what that reunion will be like. As MercyMe's song says, "I can only imagine what it will be like" when we become a part of God's heavenly table.

Read the words of MercyMe's song and describe what God's table looks like to you. How do you see God's people coming together in ways that reflect our position as heirs to God's Kingdom? Respond below.

PRAYER
Heavenly Father, thank You for making me Your heir. Help me know how to share that inheritance with others. Amen.

RELATING TO OTHERS
Week 35: *Unified Together*
I AM BETTER THAN YOU Ephesians 2:11-12

Therefore, remember that formerly you who are Gentiles by birth and called "uncircumcised" by those who call themselves "the circumcision" (which is done in the body by human hands) — Remember that at that time you were separate from Christ, excluded from citizenship in Israel and foreigners to the covenants of the promise, without hope and without God in the world.

Most of us have experienced the pain of being left out, or not chosen, or made to feel like we don't belong. The pain can start early on a playground when teams are chosen and we're not wanted. Or, it can happen in college when we rush for a fraternity and are not picked up. It can happen throughout adulthood, when we're overlooked, passed over, or left out. It's never easy to know that you're not wanted or valued by another.

When Paul wrote to the church at Ephesus, he recognized that some people (who had been Jews before they were Christians) were making others (who were Gentiles) feel like something was wrong with them. These Jewish Christians were judging the Gentile Christians based on circumstances that they had not chosen for themselves—to be circumcised as part of the Jewish faith. For the Jewish Christians, the lack of circumcision made these Gentile Christians devalued and unaccepted. But Paul reminded the Gentile Christians how important they were to Christ because they had been given salvation through Him alone.

Are Christians still guilty of judging where others stand before God? Why? How can judging others destroy Christian unity? Respond below.

PRAYER
Heavenly Father, help me to see Your work in all people. Please stop me from ever thinking that I know You better than anyone else. Amen.

RELATING TO OTHERS
Week 35: *Unified Together*

BECOMING ONE
Ephesians 2:13–15

But now in Christ Jesus you who once were far away have been brought near by the blood of Christ. For he himself is our peace, who has made the two groups one and has destroyed the barrier, the dividing wall of hostility, by setting aside in his flesh the law with its commands and regulations. His purpose was to create in himself one new humanity out of the two, thus making peace.

Both my mother-in-law and father-in-law were widowed when they met. Both had children and grandchildren from their first marriages. In fact, the day they married they had five grandchildren between them who were all five years old. Holiday celebrations became huge and chaotic as these two families, each with their own histories and traditions, became one. Over the years, these two families have come together in unity to celebrate, to rejoice, and even to grieve.

Paul didn't just want the divisions within the church in Ephesus to be nice to each other, he wanted them to be able to put their differences aside so they could become united in the one thing they had in common—their salvation through Christ Jesus. Paul described that union as becoming "one new humanity," a union that could only happen because of the work of Jesus.

What divisions do you see in your family? In your church? What would it take for these divisions to be healed? Reread these verses again, focusing on the words "the dividing walls of hostility." What would it take to remove those in your family or your church? Respond below.

PRAYER
Heavenly Father, show us how we allow differences of opinions and ideas to become walls between us. Show me what I can do to begin to remove any walls that divide us. Amen.

RELATING TO OTHERS
Week 35: *Unified Together*
THE WAY BACK TO GOD — Ephesians 2:16–18

And in one body to reconcile both of them to God through the cross, by which he put to death their hostility. He came and preached peace to you who were far away and peace to those who were near. For through him we both have access to the Father by one Spirit.

How many non-Christians do you know? As a minister, I spend most of my time working with Christians within the church. It's when I get outside the church that I have the opportunity to meet those who haven't experienced God's salvation. If it weren't for things like soccer games, Boy Scout meetings, or my hiking club, I could live out my life within a Christian bubble. If I did, though, I would have difficulty encountering those who are far from God.

Paul emphasized that Christ came to give us all a way back to God. That means Christ came for the Jews and the Gentiles. He came for those who are still far from God just as He came for those of us who have already found our way to Him. Our access to God is not because of anything we did and is all because of what Christ did. When we truly recognize what that means, we will begin to have a burden for those who haven't yet found their way to God.

Who helped you find your way to God? What was that experience like? After you respond below, pray that God will show you those that need your help in finding their way to Him as well.

PRAYER
Heavenly Father, thank You for bringing me back to You. Help me see those whom I can help find You, too. Amen.

RELATING TO OTHERS
Week 35: *Unified Together*
WE BELONG
Ephesians 2:19–20

Consequently, you are no longer foreigners and strangers, but fellow citizens with God's people and also members of his household, built on the foundation of the apostles and prophets, with Christ Jesus himself as the chief cornerstone.

Coming home for a weekend from college was always a treat. My mom knew what food I liked and had made my favorites for dinner and stuffed the cabinets with my favorite snacks. My dad gave me his undivided attention as he asked about school and listened to my stories. My friends were always welcome, as well. Coming home was always special. I felt special there. I belonged.

Paul reminded the groups at Ephesus who were struggling with their differences and their opinions of each other that they all belonged to God's household. They were all part of His family. They belonged to Him. That meant they also belonged to each other. Not only did they all belong to God, but they were part of the faith that had come from Christ and had been taught by the apostles and the prophets. They belonged to the church that Christ Jesus had founded.

Our citizenship is the same as those who received Paul's original letter. We belong to God. We are a part of His family. And we are a part of the church that was created through Christ Jesus. What does that legacy mean to you personally? To the church corporately? Respond below.

PRAYER
Heavenly Father, thank You for allowing me to be a part of Your household. Help me to be worthy of that position in the way I relate to others. Amen.

RELATING TO OTHERS
Week 35: *Unified Together*
LIVING AS A TEMPLE
Ephesians 2:21–22

In him the whole building is joined together and rises to become a holy temple in the Lord. And in him you too are being built together to become a dwelling in which God lives by his Spirit.

Several years ago, we had the opportunity to visit the Parthenon in Athens, Greece. As I stood before that enormous building, I couldn't help but think of Paul's courageous words to the Greeks: "God doesn't live in any building that you could make yourselves." The words are my rough interpretation, but accurately reflect what I was thinking at the time. God is too great to ever be contained in anything we can do.

I wonder if Paul was thinking of his words at the Parthenon as he wrote to the church at Ephesus, another city that was famous for the Temple of Artemis, one of the seven wonders of the ancient world. Paul wanted to make sure his readers understood that the temple that ruled over their city was nothing but an empty building built by men. God prefers a different type of temple—one that is based upon the foundation of Jesus Christ and is built within the hearts of His people.

It can be easier to look to a temple or even a church building as the place we go to encounter God, rather than accepting that we are His temple. We are what others see that reflect God. We are the ones who represent Him. Those who know us may possibly only know God through what they see in us. What does that mean to you at this moment? Respond below.

PRAYER
Heavenly Father, I'm overwhelmed that You chose to reside within me. Help me live in a way that is worthy of You. Amen.

RELATING TO OTHERS
Week 36: *Mutual Respect*
DON'T TELL ME WHAT TO DO — Ephesians 5:21

Submit to one another out of reverence for Christ.

As a parent, one of the complaints I heard most often from our children was that one had tried to boss the other around. The usual response, just before an all-out fight ensued, was, "You can't tell me what to do. You're not the boss of me." Sound familiar? There's something innate in each of us that doesn't want to be bossed around by someone else. Being bossed around makes us feel small and under-valued.

In our society, *submission* has become defined as "giving in" or "being weak." Few of us want to be seen as weak or as a pushover. However, Paul explained that the act of submission is one that is voluntary, not forced or required, and is based on the true character of the Holy Spirit who dwells within us. The Spirit reflects the gentleness and humility of Christ. Should we reflect anything less?

Spend a few minutes reflecting on the idea of *submission*. Is submission a way of life for you? Do you resent being told what to do? Do you accept the call to be submissive before God? Respond below.

PRAYER
Heavenly Father, help me bend my will to Yours. Help me learn that submission is a holy act, not one of weakness. Amen.

RELATING TO OTHERS
Week 36: *Mutual Respect*
WHO'S THE BOSS
Ephesians 5:22-24

Wives, submit yourselves to your own husbands as you do to the Lord. For the husband is the head of the wife as Christ is the head of the church, his body, of which he is the Savior. Now as the church submits to Christ, so also wives should submit to their husbands in everything.

The act of *submission* has become a hot topic, especially for couples preparing their wedding celebrations. Many brides have chosen to leave out the word "obey" because they want to be seen as an equal partner. The wedding covenant has become reflective of the way the couple wants their marriage to operate.

The difficulty with that is God has designed a specific relationship to create the strongest working bond between a married couple. And that relationship is based on the willingness to submit to one another. Women have often heard sermons on these verses in isolation, being lead to believe that submission is only required of them. However, Paul used these verses to instruct the wife about her role in a marital relationship before he moved on to describe the husband's submissive role as well. God's plan only works when both partners voluntarily choose to submit to each other. Maybe one reason so many marriages fail is that one or both partners are not willing to accept their role in submitting to the other.

Below, describe your understanding of the biblical role of a woman in marriage. If you're married, use that description to look at your marriage. If you're not married, consider how you've seen this biblical role in marriages you've witnessed.

PRAYER
Heavenly Father, help me learn to be submissive to my spouse and my family. Teach me to see a submissive attitude as a sign of strength instead of weakness. Amen.

RELATING TO OTHERS
Week 36: *Mutual Respect*
LOVE LIKE CHRIST
Ephesians 5:25-33

Husbands, love your wives, just as Christ loved the church and gave himself up for her to make her holy, cleansing her by the washing with water through the word, and to present her to himself as a radiant church, without stain or wrinkle or any other blemish, but holy and blameless. In this same way, husbands ought to love their wives as their own bodies. He who loves his wife loves himself. After all, no one ever hated their own body, but they feed and care for their body, just as Christ does the church—for we are members of his body. "For this reason a man will leave his father and mother and be united to his wife, and the two will become one flesh." This is a profound mystery—but I am talking about Christ and the church. However, each one of you also must love his wife as he loves himself, and the wife must respect her husband.

I recently heard a radio commercial for divorce attorneys. The ad featured a wife who shared that there was no love in her marriage. So, she asks, "If the love is gone, there's no reason for the marriage to continue, is there?" Our culture thinks of love only as an emotion, a feeling that makes the pulse race a little, and maybe a knot is felt in the stomach. It's all about feelings.

Jesus demonstrated a different type of love...a love that was completely sacrificial, a love that puts others first, a love that demonstrated the love of God. And it was this type of love—the deep self-denying, totally incorporating love—that Paul put forth for husbands to model. This is not a love that is bossy or overbearing. It is not a love that demands respect or obedience. It is a love that models the love of Christ in all things. Feelings can come and go, but to love a spouse as Christ loved His church is a constant that has to be experienced to be understood.

Below, describe the love of Christ that should be demonstrated to a spouse in marriage. How could that type of love change the way our culture perceives Christian marriage?

PRAYER
Heavenly Father, thank You for the love of Christ. Help me learn to love others, especially my spouse and my family, with love that models the love He has shown me. Amen.

RELATING TO OTHERS
Week 36: *Mutual Respect*
HONORING A PARENT
Ephesians 6:1-4

Children, obey your parents in the Lord, for this is right. "Honor your father and mother"—which is the first commandment with a promise—"so that it may go well with you and that you may enjoy long life on the earth." Fathers, do not exasperate your children; instead, bring them up in the training and instruction of the Lord.

In my work with senior adults, I've had the opportunity to observe the relationships between senior adults and their grown children. Probably the most beautiful example I've seen is between a daughter and her mother. The widowed mother is now wheelchair bound. Yet she continues to maintain a productive life as her daughter helps her get to appointments, Bible studies, and book clubs. It is a beautiful example of honoring a parent. The daughter's words are humbling. "Mama took care of me when I needed her," she says. "Why would I do less for her now?"

Sadly, this beautiful picture of an adult child honoring a parent is not the norm. Unfortunately, many more senior adults have little, if any, relationship with their children. It is true that when senior adult parents need their children the most is also the time when those adult children have the busiest and most demanding lives. Yet, the biblical picture is the same as the daughter's words above, "Why would we not respond to the needs of our parents now?"

Consider your relationship with your parents. How do you honor their lives with your involvement today? If you were to defend your actions, would you have enough evidence for others to recognize how you honor your parents? Respond below.

PRAYER
Heavenly Father, thank You for my parents. Help me remember the things they have done over the years in my life. Convict me when I fail to give them the honor and respect they deserve. Amen.

RELATING TO OTHERS
Week 36: *Mutual Respect*

MORE LIKE JESUS
Ephesians 6:5–9

Slaves, obey your earthly masters with respect and fear, and with sincerity of heart, just as you would obey Christ. Obey them not only to win their favor when their eye is on you, but as slaves of Christ, doing the will of God from your heart. Serve wholeheartedly, as if you were serving the Lord, not people, because you know that the Lord will reward each one for whatever good they do, whether they are slave or free. And masters, treat your slaves in the same way. Do not threaten them, since you know that he who is both their Master and yours is in heaven, and there is no favoritism with him.

The history of slavery is still an uncomfortable one in the United States as well as throughout the world. It is hard to understand how anyone ever felt he had the right to own another individual. As Christians, it can be difficult to read Paul's words about how slaves should act and be treated in the Bible. It could never have been seen as a relationship that God approved, could it?

Paul's words don't approve or condemn the institution of slavery. His words remind us of the importance of relationships between people, of the way people treat others, and of God's expectations for our actions. While in the first-century world, slavery was an accepted, even honored, practice, it's easy to understand that any time one person has control over another, the possibility for mistreatment and abuse exists. Therefore, Paul's words can still speak to us today. As Christians who have received the grace and salvation of Jesus Christ, how we treat others matters.

Who has control of your career or your children or even your finances? Reread the verses above, inserting that name in place of each use of "masters." How should you respond to that person who controls you? Do the same thing with the person(s) who are under your control (such as employees), inserting his or her name in place of "slaves." Below, record what you've learned about yourself and how you should respond to others.

PRAYER
Heavenly Father, teach me to be more like Jesus. Help me be a little more like Him every day. Amen.

DISCIPLING OTHERS
Week 37: *Teach By Example*

SET AN EXAMPLE
1 Timothy 4:11-12

Command and teach these things. Don't let anyone look down on you because you are young, but set an example for the believers in speech, in conduct, in love, in faith and in purity.

My early days in ministry were not always easy. I had a lot to learn and little experience under my belt upon which to draw. Even worse, I looked younger than I really was. It took time to gain the experience and skills I needed to deserve the trust of the parents of the teenagers I had been entrusted to guide.

Paul's mentee Timothy was between the age of twenty and thirty, an age that didn't garner respect in the first century, when he received Paul's admonition not to let any one look down upon him for his youth or inexperience. Timothy must have felt some of the same emotions I felt starting out. But, we also had something in common—we had both responded to a unique calling to ministry, a calling that included specific expectations. However, the exhortation of Paul's words is the same for young and old Christians. We are called to set an example—an example that reflects the One we follow in what we say (in both content and vocabulary), the way we act, and in our faith. It can be difficult to convince people of our faith in Christ when our lifestyles don't reflect who He is and what He has done for us. It's just that simple.

Does your life reflect whom you follow? How? Consider your speech—the words you use and the way you speak. Do these reflect Christ or something else? Consider your actions in the same way. Are these areas in your life reflecting things other than Christ? Respond below.

PRAYER
Heavenly Father, I know that I let You down in my words, my attitudes, and my actions. Convict me when I let You down. Help me focus on learning to reflect You in all I do and all I am. Amen.

DISCIPLING OTHERS
Week 37: *Teach By Example*
BE DEVOTED TO THE WORD   1 Timothy 4:13

Until I come, devote yourself to the public reading of Scripture, to preaching and to teaching.

In my trips to Jerusalem, I always enjoy being at the Western Wall, a place that is sacred to the Jews. They gather there when they are troubled and when they are celebrating; when they need to pray; and to hear the public reading of Scripture. I've watched as a rabbi opens an elaborately decorated case, pulls out a sacred scroll, and begins to read from the Scripture. His actions and his words garner the attention of all who are in the area.

Paul's words to Timothy are especially important to those who are called to vocational ministry, but they have value for all believers. We cannot disciple others without using the Scripture. And if we're not studying Scripture for ourselves, there is no way we can adequately preach or teach it to others. Far too often, people try to teach others how to follow Christ using faulty information or biblical myths. The most important thing we can do in our walk is to spend time in studying God's Word and then passing on what we're learning to others.

I've occasionally heard someone say that he or she didn't need to study the Bible any longer because they've already read it. How would you respond if you heard that comment? Does your life reflect how important the Bible is? Why? Respond below.

PRAYER
Heavenly Father, You have given us Your Word so we may know You and know how to follow You. Help me continue to learn, to have a desire within me for Your Word and for sharing that Word with others. Amen.

DISCIPLING OTHERS
Week 37: *Teach By Example*
USE YOUR GIFT
1 Timothy 4:14

Do not neglect your gift, which was given you through prophecy when the body of elders laid their hands on you.

I'm pretty practical when it comes to giving gifts. I try to give things that I believe will be used. To do that, I have to figure out what's important to the one who will receive the gift—what are the interests, the needs, the wants—that I can meet. The gifts may not be pretty, but they reflect my understanding of the one who will receive the gift.

Likewise as Christians, we receive the gift of the Holy Spirit. God knew what we needed in order to live as His people, and He gifted us with the Spirit who can guide us in that process. Paul reminded Timothy that he had also received that gift. Beyond this statement, there is no biblical record of the experience of the elders laying their hands upon Timothy. It must have been much like an ordination service today, when deacons and elders lay their hands upon a ministerial candidate in prayer for the candidate's ministry journey. We may not all experience this type of ceremony, but we all receive the gift of the Holy Spirit to guide our way.

How do you recognize the Holy Spirit in your life? Do you depend upon His presence? How? Have you neglected or ignored His presence? Why? Respond below.

PRAYER
Heavenly Father, thank You for Your gift of the Holy Spirit, and for knowing what I would need in my journey of faith. Help me stay in touch with the Spirit. Don't allow me to ignore or neglect Him. Amen.

DISCIPLING OTHERS
Week 37: *Teach By Example*

SLOW AND STEADY
1 Timothy 4:15

Be diligent in these matters; give yourself wholly to them, so that everyone may see your progress.

I'm a runner. I have been most of my adult life. I run most days during my lunch break, or if that doesn't work, I run after I get home. Running keeps me in shape, and helps me handle stress. When I don't get to run, I don't feel right. Running has become a part of me. Studies have shown that if a runner skips only three days of training, he or she will begin to lose some of the progress that's already been made. A runner has to be diligent in making time for running, or he will become someone who likes to run occasionally. There's a big difference in the two.

Paul reminded Timothy to be diligent in the living out of his faith. Diligence has been defined as a steady, earnest, and energetic effort. It describes my running and it describes how we are to approach our faith journey. The faith journey should be a steady, day-by-day process in which we earnestly seek to know God better. That kind of progress will be evident to the people who know us and see our lives.

Think about your faith journey. Is it steady? Is it earnest? Is it energetic? Below, evaluate your journey using these questions. Then, consider areas in which your journey cannot be described by these characteristics. How does your faith journey strengthen or hinder how others see you as a person of faith? Why?

PRAYER
Heavenly Father, help me become diligent in the way I study You. Help me be steady in my journey. And help me be energetic in sharing my journey with others. Amen.

DISCIPLING OTHERS
Week 37: *Teach By Example*
BE YOUR FAITH
1 Timothy 4:16

Watch your life and doctrine closely. Persevere in them, because if you do, you will save both yourself and your hearers.

I'm not a fan of reality TV, but my wife is. Often, I get stuck in the room with some show on TV that she's watching because of the glimpse it gives to the way people act and react to others. Recently we watched a show on religious cults, which were based verbally on the message of love in the Scripture. However, the way the cults lived out that love were anything but reflective of what love and relationship mean to God. The cults' actions didn't match the doctrine they claimed to follow.

Our society has become used to people who claim one thing and do something else. Open any newspaper or magazine to find stories of celebrities, politicians, teachers, ministers—yes, even Christians—who verbally pronounce the things they believe in and hold dear but cannot live up too. Is it any wonder that many non-Christians watch Christians and stay confused about what Christianity is all about? Paul's admonition to Timothy is important to us as well. What we truly believe is seen in the way we live. If our lives do not demonstrate our faith and trust in God, it is not difficult to understand that our actions would not attract non-believers to the One we claim to follow.

Think of some of your models in faith. How do their lives reflect what they believe about God? Can others say the same about you? Why or why not?

PRAYER
Heavenly Father, I know that it can be difficult to get my attention sometimes, but I ask that You convict me when my attitudes and actions fail to demonstrate who You are. Amen.

DISCIPLING OTHERS
Week 38: *Testify to the Gospel*
UNASHAMED
2 Timothy 1:8

So do not be ashamed of the testimony about our Lord or of me his prisoner. Rather, join with me in suffering for the gospel, by the power of God.

When my wife's mother was cleaning out boxes before a move, she found a letter that had been sent to her just after she had given birth to her first child—my wife. The letter was from her father and it was a deeply intimate message of encouragement and faith. The letter is now in my wife's hands and is an historical reminder of the generations of faith in her family.

Paul's exhortations to Timothy in this second letter are also deeply intimate and personal. Paul was already imprisoned in Rome, already suffering physically in that imprisonment. While Paul was allowed a time of house arrest in Rome, it is believed that he also spent time in the dark, dank underground Mamertine Prison. Many died in that prison from starvation or strangulation. Yet, Philippians 1:13 records that all the prison guards of the Praetorian knew that Paul suffered for his Christ. When Paul encouraged Timothy to be unashamed to share his testimony, Paul knew what it could cost Timothy. Yet for Paul, any other response to Christ would be too costly spiritually.

Are you ashamed of the gospel? Do you take the opportunity to share your testimony, regardless of possible consequences? Why? Reflect on your testimony below and prayerfully seek ways to stand unashamed before others.

PRAYER
Heavenly Father, help me be strong as I share my testimony—both through my words and through my life—with others. Help me keep my focus on You. Amen.

DISCIPLING OTHERS
Week 38: *Testify to the Gospel*
GRACE RECEIVED
2 Timothy 1:9a

He has saved us and called us to a holy life—not because of anything we have done but because of his own purpose and grace.

The birth of our first child helped me understand God's grace from a new perspective. There was this beautiful, dark haired infant that we had created. As beautiful as he was, he didn't do anything but eat and poop and allow us to love him. He loudly let us know when he needed something, but it was awhile before we received anything emotionally back from him. And we loved him...completely, totally, passionately. In fact, our world evolved around him and our love for him. That love was made even more special when our son was able to demonstrate and verbalize that he loved us back. Even if he had never been able to show us his love, we would love him still.

Paul reminded Timothy of that kind of grace from God that was not based on anything we did but totally based on His ability to love us. Our salvation comes from God out of His purpose and His grace. And that grace comes with an expectation—that we will live holy lives.

What does the concept of "grace" mean to you? How have you experienced God's grace in your life? How would you explain God's grace to a non-believer? Respond below.

PRAYER
Heavenly Father, help me remember that I am Yours and that I'm covered by Your grace. Remind me that I did nothing to earn that grace and that there's nothing I could do that would help me earn that grace. Amen.

_____

_____

_____

_____

_____

DISCIPLING OTHERS
Week 38: *Testify to the Gospel*
IT'S BEEN REVEALED 2 Timothy 1:9b–10

This grace was given us in Christ Jesus before the beginning of time, but it has now been revealed through the appearing of our Savior, Christ Jesus, who has destroyed death and has brought life and immortality to light through the gospel.

Reality television is often based on keeping viewers interested until the "Big Reveal" at the end. It doesn't matter if it's how a room is redecorated, or which Jeopardy contestant has the right answer to the final question, or which bachelor is chosen as a long-term companion. In each case, dramatic tension is created until that final revelation. The "Big Reveal" usually leads to a ratings success, not to mention a profitable season.

Unfortunately, the overuse of the concept of the "Big Reveal" can lead us to become numb to the impact of the true "Big Reveal" that is seen through the life, death, and resurrection of Jesus. The word *revelation* can be understood as making something once hidden now visible. Paul described the revelation of Christ's grace as having had its beginning before time began and its fulfillment in the life of Christ. We only understand God's plan through the death and resurrection. Now that's a "Big Reveal."

Below, describe what is revealed about God through His Son's death and resurrection. Prayerfully consider how that revelation can be explained to a non-believer.

PRAYER
Heavenly Father, don't let me take for granted the fact that Your plan, from the beginning of time, was to send Your Son to bring me to You. Thank You for that gift and for the way that gift also helps me understand how much You love me. Amen.

_____

_____

_____

_____

_____

DISCIPLING OTHERS
Week 38: *Testify to the Gospel*

HERALDING THE NEWS
2 Timothy 1:11

And of this gospel I was appointed a herald and an apostle and a teacher.

When's the last time you had to deal with a car salesman? They know their best chance of closing a deal is the first time they meet you, so they tend to be a little pushy trying to make a deal. Most of us don't like that "in our face" pressure and we quickly respond, "Thanks, but we're just looking." We don't want to commit before we're ready.

Paul used three words to explain what he was called to do—he was to be a *herald*, to be an apostle, and to be a teacher. Paul often referred to himself as an apostle because Jesus personally called him on the Damascus road. And he spent much of his time helping establish new congregations, and teaching the leaders and the members in person and through his letters. But he also took the responsibility of being God's *herald*—the one who was given the responsibility to announce important news for God. In fact, he felt driven to get to Rome so he could share that message with Caesar. Paul knew that the gospel message he had to share was the most important message that could be delivered.

To what has God called you? How do you fulfill that calling? Is sharing God's message a part of that calling? Why? Respond below.

PRAYER
Heavenly Father, help me share Your message with all I meet. Remind me that what I know as a disciple of Christ is more important that any other message others will ever hear. Amen.

DISCIPLING OTHERS
Week 38: *Testify to the Gospel*
DEPOSITED IN SAFETY
2 Timothy 1:12

That is why I am suffering as I am. Yet this is no cause for shame, because I know whom I have believed, and am convinced that he is able to guard what I have entrusted to him until that day.

We grew up hearing stories of what our grandparents had experienced during the Great Depression. When the stock market and banks collapsed, our grandparents and their families suffered. They struggled to live. And they lost their trust in institutions. Even with the safeguards established by the federal government, many never regained their trust enough to put everything they had into a bank for safekeeping.

Paul reminded Timothy that complete trust could be placed in God. Paul entrusted his present situation and his future to God alone, in spite of the current suffering he was experiencing. He understood that only God was worthy of that kind of trust. Paul had given his faith, his commitment, even his very life to God. As he wrote to Timothy, Paul wanted him to understand the depth of his commitment and trust in God. He expected no less from Timothy as well.

Paul never expected Timothy to do anything that he (Paul) had not already done. What have you given to God? Can you explain that to a non-believer? Or to a new believer? What difference has that made in your life? Respond below.

PRAYER
Heavenly Father, You are everything. I am nothing without You. Help me to rest in confidence and safety in You. Amen.

DISCIPLING OTHERS
Week 39: *Teaching What is Right*
TEACH SALVATION FOR ALL　　Titus 2:11

For the grace of God has appeared that offers salvation to all people.

Most churches have a mission statement...a statement that defines what is most important to that local congregation. Read a sampling of them and you'll find one principal in common—that the congregation is based upon the grace they've received through the death and resurrection of Jesus Christ, a salvation that is available to all people. It is the defining thought of who we are as Christians. And it is the one thing we cannot accomplish on our own.

Titus had been a friend and trusted companion to Paul in several of his missionary journeys. Titus was so trusted that Paul left him on the island of Crete to begin the work of establishing churches there. But Paul didn't leave Titus there and forget him. Instead, Paul wrote Titus to remind him what was most important in his work there. In the face of false teachers, Paul wanted to remind Titus to make sure that nothing was done that compromised the accurate message of Christ's grace available to all.

Imagine that you are sitting with someone who is not a believer who has asked you what you believe about Christ and why that belief is important to you. Answer that question below and then compare your answer to Paul's writing in Titus 2:11–3:2.

PRAYER
Heavenly Father, help me know how to talk about my faith with others. Convict me when I communicate things that are inaccurate or false about You. Amen.

_____

_____

_____

_____

DISCIPLING OTHERS
Week 39: *Teaching What is Right*
WHAT WE LEARN FROM GRACE — Titus 2:12

It teaches us to say "No" to ungodliness and worldly passions, and to live self-controlled, upright and godly lives in this present age...

When our son was fifteen, he came home from a shopping trip with a music CD that had a warning label on the cover. When we reviewed the lyrics of the songs on the album, we were shocked by the content and the profanity. When confronted, he tried to slough off the offensive material, saying it was no big deal because all the teenagers were listening to it. Our question for him was, "But as a Christian, how should your faith impact the choices you make, regardless of what other teenagers do?" It took about twenty-four hours before he came to us with an apology and a new understanding of what his faith required of him.

Paul reminded Titus that the grace we've received through Christ teaches us how not to be drawn into the ungodliness and worldliness of those around us. But it doesn't remove us from the society in which those flourish. Rather, God's grace allows us to live in that world but to be different from the world. Living differently than those around us becomes a clear picture of Christ's transformational act in our lives.

Below, describe how your faith causes your life to be different from those around you. Why does the way you live out your faith become important to those who do not know Jesus?

PRAYER
Heavenly Father, show me where my lifestyle conflicts with my faith in You. Help me live my life in a way that brings You glory. Amen.

DISCIPLING OTHERS
Week 39: *Teaching What is Right*
LIVE IN HOPE
Titus 2:13-14

While we wait for the blessed hope—the appearing of the glory of our great God and Savior, Jesus Christ, who gave himself for us to redeem us from all wickedness and to purify for himself a people that are his very own, eager to do what is good.

Our days living on a seminary campus were good ones for us. We felt wrapped up in a safe cocoon with others who shared our faith and our values. We studied and worked and established relationships, all knowing that we were there for only a short time. We knew that our future lay in God's hands and waited with anticipation to see where that future would take us.

As Christians, our future rests in God's hands...and in that time when we will join Christ in eternity. Therefore, the lives we lead while we wait are temporary but significant. We can wait with anticipation for that day when our lives come to fulfillment in Christ Jesus. Peter described the way we should live this way: "Dear friends, I urge you, as foreigners and exiles, to abstain from sinful desires, which wage war against your soul. Live such good lives among the pagans that, though they accuse you of doing wrong, they may see your good deeds and glorify God on the day he visits us" (1 Peter 3:11-12).

Describe how you are anticipating your future eternity with Christ below. Are you anticipating it eagerly? Does the future frighten you? Or, are you too overwhelmed with living now that you don't think much about the future?

PRAYER
Heavenly Father, let me rest in the promise of my future with You throughout eternity. Help me make decisions in this life based on Your promise for my future. Amen.

DISCIPLING OTHERS
Week 39: *Teaching What is Right*

TEACH WHAT'S IMPORTANT
Titus 2:15

These, then, are the things you should teach. Encourage and rebuke with all authority. Do not let anyone despise you.

In a recent Bible study with senior adults, one of the members who had been a Bible teacher since the age of 14 was asked what that responsibility throughout her life had been like. She responded, "It was a blessing. I always learned more than I could possibly teach. But it was a responsibility to make sure that what I taught was accurate." Now 90 and with some health problems, she no longer teaches. But she continues to study, to learn, and to challenge herself with the Word of God.

Teaching others the Bible is a huge responsibility. A biblical teacher should rebuke with discernment without being critical or judgmental. And in all things, a biblical teacher should be encouraging, all while standing on the authority of the Scripture. That can only happen with a teacher who is a student of Scripture who seeks God's heart. As Paul wrote to young Timothy, "Do your best to present yourself as one approved, a worker who does not need to be ashamed and who correctly handles the word of truth" (2 Timothy 2:15).

What skills have you learned for studying Scripture correctly? How can you be sure that what you teach or study is handled correctly? How would you help another believer to understand what it means to handle God's Word correctly? Respond below.

PRAYER
Heavenly Father, teach me how to study Your Word passionately. Create within me a desire to know Your Word. Amen.

DISCIPLING OTHERS
Week 39: *Teaching What is Right*

BE DIFFERENT THAN OTHERS Titus 3:1-2

Remind the people to be subject to rulers and authorities, to be obedient, to be ready to do whatever is good, to slander no one, to be peaceable and considerate, and always to be gentle toward everyone.

My mother was the daughter of a pastor. She grew up recognizing the special authority a pastor had, by virtue of his divine calling to ministry and his unique calling to minister in the local church. For her, those two callings made him the authoritative leader of the church. Those two callings still exist for all those in the ministry.

Paul concluded this section of his letter to Titus with specifics of how Christians were to act. He stated that they were to be submissive and obedient to political authorities, and to be gentle and considerate to all. Today, people of authority are found both within and outside the church. And few people easily submit to those in authority. Yet, Paul once again reminded Titus, and now us, that the actions of believers are supposed to be different from others. While others rebel, believers are called to be obedient and peaceable. While others look after their own desires, believers are called to be considerate and gentle. Paul would be the first to remind us that following God's expectations is not easy. These expectations are what make us different from non-believers.

In the verses printed above, underline the words Paul used to describe the characteristics believers are to exhibit. Then, in the space below, prayerfully consider how those characteristics are present or absent in your life.

PRAYER
Heavenly Father, help me remember that I am held to a different standard of behavior than those who don't know You. Help me develop those characteristics that are so unlike me, or that I personally don't value. Amen.

_____

_____

_____

_____

_____

DISCIPLING OTHERS
Week 40: *Serve the World/Love Others*
IN MY PRAYERS Philemon 4

I always thank my God as I remember you in my prayers.

My wife's foot surgery was more serious than we had expected. We expected her recovery to take weeks. It took months. She was mostly homebound with limited mobility, cut off from friends, and left alone for hours as I had to leave her to work. It was a discouraging time for her. But she was overwhelmed at the number of cards and phone calls, reminding her of the prayers that were being lifted for her. After two months in recovery with no end in sight, her Sunday School class requested that a prayer quilt be made for her so she would have a tangible reminder of those prayers. Those prayers meant everything to her.

Personal prayers for another are an indication of a relationship, one made intimate because of the presence of God as a part of it. Paul knew Philemon. Paul prayed for Philemon and thanked God for him. As he wrote to Philemon, Paul reminded him of their relationship and his prayers. Paul's request of Philemon was bathed in prayer and thanksgiving.

Christian theologian C.S. Lewis explained why prayer was a part of his life: "I pray because I can't help myself. I pray because I'm helpless. I pray because the need flows out of me all the time, waking and sleeping. It doesn't change God, it changes me." How have you been blessed through the long-term prayers of others? How have you prayed for others over a period of time? Below, record what God taught you through the experience.

PRAYER
Heavenly Father, thank You for prayer—for allowing me to come before You. Teach me to pray as You would want me to pray. Amen.

DISCIPLING OTHERS
Week 40: *Serve the World/Love Others*
I HEARD ABOUT YOUR LOVE
Philemon 5

Because I hear about your love for all his holy people and your faith in the Lord Jesus..

In our early days of parenthood, I had to be out of town for conferences and retreats. With no cell phones or internet, and expensive long-distance phone charges, I couldn't wait to get home to catch up on what our children had been up to. I would hear both the good and the bad. Obviously, the good things were much easier to hear than the bad. And knowing that things were going well without me allowed me to do the things that my ministry position required.

Paul was in prison in Rome when he wrote to Philemon. Paul was cut off from most of the churches he had started and relied upon letters and testimonies from those who came to see him to tell him what was happening in those churches. Imagine the joy that he must have experienced when the testimonies of faith were shared with him. Because of what he knew about Philemon and had heard about him while imprisoned, Paul could write to him with a personal request. The foundation for that letter was their shared faith in Jesus Christ as Lord.

How is your faith demonstrated for others to see? Do they see your love? Or, do they see unloving characteristics? Respond below.

PRAYER
Heavenly Father, help me see myself as I am seen by others. Convict me when I fail to show others Your love. Teach me how to live in a way that honors You. Amen.

DISCIPLING OTHERS
Week 40: *Serve the World/Love Others*
IT'S A PARTNERSHIP
Philemon 6a

I pray that your partnership with us in the faith may be effective in deepening your understanding of every good thing we share for the sake of Christ.

My wife is a fan of *Dancing with the Stars*, so I've watched more couples dance together than I like to admit. While it's not a preference for me, it is interesting to watch partnerships form between the dancers. The strength of the dancers' partnership, and the success of the partnership, becomes dependent upon the partners' ability to work together.

Paul reminded Philemon that they were partners in faith with a common goal, that of being effective in ministry. Paul was singularly focused on completing his ministry assignment. He recognized the need for others to partner with him so that ministry would be effective. In this one verse, Paul highlighted two ideas—the partnership of the body working together, and the spiritual growth that comes from that partnership.

As we mature in our faith, we are able to do things we could not have done as an immature believer. Such was the basis of Paul's letter to Philemon. As we mature, we are expected to be able to treat others more like Christ has treated us. What growth have you seen in your ability to respond to others? Respond below.

PRAYER
Heavenly Father, help me daily to grow in You—in my actions and in my understanding of You. Amen.

DISCIPLING OTHERS
Week 40: *Serve the World/Love Others*
A DEEPENING UNDERSTANDING Philemon 6b

I pray that your partnership with us in the faith may be effective in deepening your understanding of every good thing we share for the sake of Christ.

I started out in ministry working with teenagers. I loved being a part of their spiritual journey as they began to examine and question what they believed. I'm ending my ministry time working with senior adults. I love being a part of their spiritual journey as well as they continue to dig into the Scripture, continue to learn about the character of God, and continue to grow in their faith. Both of these groups are generally at different places in their spiritual journeys. Both continue to grow in their understanding of God and what their belief in Him means in their lives.

That process of growing in faith, of an ever-deepening understanding of God, is the journey of discipleship. The process of discipleship is like that of a river. From the time we accept our salvation through Jesus Christ, our lives will never be the same. We will constantly and continually be changed in the process. Paul described that process with the words "deepening in your understanding of every good thing we share." Our faith can only be deepened when we study God's Word, when we challenge our premises and assumptions in light of that study, and when we willingly change the way we respond to what we learn.

Below, describe how you understood God when you first became a believer. Then, describe how you understand God now. How has your understanding changed? How would you describe your spiritual journey to a new believer? Would your journey encourage a new believer? Why?

PRAYER
Heavenly Father, challenge my beliefs. Deepen my understanding of all that has come to my life because of You. Amen.

DISCIPLING OTHERS
Week 40: *Serve the World/Love Others*
FOR CHRIST'S SAKE
Philemon 6c

I pray that your partnership with us in the faith may be effective in deepening your understanding of every good thing we share for the sake of Christ.

Christian writers Rick Warren, Max Lucado, and others have reminded us that, as believers, our lives are not about us and what we want, but it's all about God and what He wants. In our ego-centric society, that's an unknown and challenging idea. Warren describes it this way: "You were born by His purpose and for His purpose." It's not about us. It's all about God.

Paul wanted Philemon to do what would be unthinkable—to give Onesimus his freedom rather than punish him as a runaway slave. And Paul's reason behind his request was about why Philemon should take this unthinkable action—Philemon's action would bring glory to God. In this one verse, Paul summed up why he could make this request of Philemon: Philemon's understanding of God and all that God had done for him would allow him to take an extreme action, and one that was not required of him, for the sake of Christ. What Paul requested was not about Philemon at all. It was about God.

Write these words below: *It's not about me. It's about God.* What does that statement mean to you? What changes would your life demonstrate if you lived according to those words? How would your life be different if you did? Respond below.

PRAYER
Heavenly Father, I know that my life is Yours and that what I do can bring glory or dishonor to You. Help me live in a way that my life is all about You. Amen.

DISCIPLING OTHERS
Week 41: *Do Good to Others*
CHECK THE LIST
1 Peter 3:8–9

Finally, all of you, be like-minded, be sympathetic, love one another, be compassionate and humble. Do not repay evil with evil or insult with insult. On the contrary, repay evil with blessing, because to this you were called so that you may inherit a blessing.

I'm a list-maker. Doesn't matter what I have to do, I will create a list for it. Sometimes, just the process of writing something on the list will be enough to help me remember something I'm supposed to do. I like lists when I'm reading as well. I like a writer who pulls out the key points and puts them in a bulleted list for emphasis. The organization of that information into a list helps me get a handle on the writer's key points.

In verse 8, Peter provided a list as well. His list is a summary of his exhortations of how to treat others and live righteously from the earlier part of this letter. He listed five commands: Live in harmony with each other; be sympathetic with each other; love each other as family members; be compassionate and kind-hearted to each other; and be humble by putting the interests of others before themselves. And while each of these commands are explained in terms of how we are to love our fellow believers, verse 9 reminds us that we have to love those who are not believers as well. Loving other believers can be challenging enough. But when we accept the responsibility to love those who are unlovable, we are faced with the uniqueness of Christ's message. We are expected to treat others in ways that are impossible without the Holy Spirit's intervention in our lives.

Write Peter's five commands below. Beside each, describe what that command means in the way you are to treat those within the church. Then, describe what it means about the way you are to treat those who are not believers. Evaluate how you're doing on both of these levels. Pray that God will give you the strength to meet the challenges of treating others the way God requires.

PRAYER
Heavenly Father, help me love others, to care about them, and to put their needs before mine. Help me treat those who are unlovable the way You would have me. Amen.

DISCIPLING OTHERS
Week 41: *Do Good to Others*

DO GOOD   1 Peter 3:10–12

For, "Whoever would love life and see good days must keep their tongue from evil and their lips from deceitful speech. They must turn from evil and do good; they must seek peace and pursue it. For the eyes of the Lord are on the righteous and his ears are attentive to their prayer, but the face of the Lord is against those who do evil."

When our teenaged children left our house, they went with the encouragement to "be good." For us, it was a reminder that who they were and how they acted mattered to us, and to them. Neither were perfect teenagers. As adults, both are involved in work that provides care for others—one is a firefighter and the other works in missions.

In verses 10-12, Peter quoted Psalm 34:12-16 in which David wrote about what God expects of His people. The psalm divides people into two groups—those who fear God and those who do not. People who fear God are required to "do good," and to do the opposite of what people who do not fear God do. Unfortunately today, the actions of those who fear God are often the same as those who do not. But God expects more from us...to watch our speech, to turn from evil, to seek peace, and to do good. Our actions become the visual definition of what we believe.

Below, describe what it means to "fear God." Then, record how fearing God impacts your speech, your actions, and your life.

PRAYER
Heavenly Father, I stand in awe before You because You are holy and righteous. Help me turn from evil and from those who would do evil. Teach me to "do good" through my life. Amen.

DISCIPLING OTHERS
Week 41: *Do Good to Others*
YOU ARE BLESSED
1 Peter 3:13–14

Who is going to harm you if you are eager to do good? But even if you should suffer for what is right, you are blessed. "Do not fear their threats; do not be frightened."

I've served in full-time ministry since 1976. For the majority of that time, it has been a blessing to be able to be involved in God's work through the local congregation. I've loved the relationships that have been developed over the years. Ministry has been a blessing for me. However, every once in a while, someone decides he or she just doesn't like me. It doesn't matter if there's a good reason for the dislike...it's just there. Once or twice, someone has really created some tension for me. It's just part of life, but it certainly wasn't fun to work through.

Peter told his readers that people would not try to hurt them if they did the right thing. But, then, he reminded them that even if that happened—if they were mistreated or even persecuted for living according to God's desire for them—they were still blessed because they belonged to God.

It feels personal when someone doesn't like us or doesn't support what we're doing. And in the midst of that tension, it can be difficult to remember how blessed we are through Christ Jesus. Yet, our hope is in Christ. That is the only thing upon which we can depend.

Think about a time when someone made it difficult for you, even though you thought you were doing the right thing. Record how the experience made you feel below. What did you learn from the experience about yourself and about your faith in God?

PRAYER
Heavenly Father, help me keep my eyes on You, even when I'm facing criticism, dislike, or persecution. Thank You for the blessing that can only come from You. Amen.

DISCIPLING OTHERS
Week 41: *Do Good to Others*

GIVE ANSWER   1 Peter 3:15a

But in your hearts revere Christ as Lord. Always be prepared to give an answer to everyone who asks you to give the reason for the hope that you have.

Our nine-year-old grandson has been asking questions about what Christianity is. One of his questions came after watching the baptism of a younger child. "She's still a big tattle-tell and a meanie," he said. "Why isn't she doing the right thing now that she's a Christian?" It was a great question. As a tangible thinker, he has trouble understanding concepts like *grace* and *hope*, and instead focuses on what he actually sees someone do.

Peter understood that non-believers will ask questions based on what they see in our lives. He encouraged his readers to be prepared to answer the tough questions that non-believers will ask based on what they've seen in our lives. He stressed the importance of being able to verbalize what we believe about Christ...about the grace and the hope of eternal life that comes through Him. Our faith can be explained with those two concepts of what Jesus Christ has done for us.

What questions have you been asked about your faith that were difficult to answer? Write these below. If you still have trouble answering them, talk through them with other believers. If you're mentoring new believers, help them formulate answers for these as well.

PRAYER
Heavenly Father, teach me how to express my faith in You in a way that can answer a non-believer's questions about You. Amen.

_____

_____

_____

_____

_____

DISCIPLING OTHERS
Week 41: *Do Good to Others*

TEACH ME
1 Peter 3:15b–16

But do this with gentleness and respect, keeping a clear conscience, so that those who speak maliciously against your good behavior in Christ may be ashamed of their slander.

In a book on clergy marriages written in the 1960s, ministers' wives were given instructions on how they should dress and act so they would not bring dishonor to their husbands. The advice given included that they should be attractive but not too much so, and well-dressed but not too expensively so. Sadly, both of these admonitions referred to the way these ministerial wives would be seen by others. The emphasis was on the outward appearance.

Peter focused on the characteristic actions that demonstrated a believer's inward presence. He used the words *gentleness* referring to our outward disposition, *respect* referring to how we treat others, and *conscience* referring to our ability to know that we're doing the right or the wrong thing. Combined, these create a picture of the person God would have us be: gentle in spirit, respectful to others, and conscious of our actions and our faults. These are godly characteristics.

Write these words below: *gentleness, respectfulness,* and *conscientious.* Describe how each of these is present in your life. Are these developing characteristics? Why? How could these become more obvious to those non-believers who only know God through you?

PRAYER
Heavenly Father, I'm not gentle all the time but I would like to be. I'm not respectful all the time but I can learn to be. I'm not always listening to my conscience but I want to. Teach me how. Amen.

_____

_____

_____

_____

_____

DISCIPLING OTHERS
Week 42: *Show Mercy*
LEGACY OF FAITH   Jude 17

But, dear friends, remember what the apostles of our Lord Jesus Christ foretold.

My earliest understanding of God came from my family. My mother's father and uncles were pastors. My father's mother was a church pianist. My parents were active ministers as well. These and other extended family members created a living stream of faith into which the next generation became a part. Except for my mother, all of these have passed on from this life. Yet, each left an indelible mark on me and on my journey of faith.

Jude identified himself as brother of James, making him a half-brother to Jesus. He had witnessed Jesus' ministry first-hand. He knew the twelve disciples who had been with Jesus throughout His ministry. He knew Paul and recognized Paul's status as an apostle of Jesus. In the face of false teachers that could destroy all that Jesus had taught, Jude reminded his readers to trust those who had known Jesus most intimately—those to whom the responsibility for the ministry had been given. Like my family members whom I learned to trust as teachers and mentors, Jude emphasized that trust in teaching had to be given to those who knew (and know) Jesus most intimately.

What does it mean to know Jesus intimately? Who are the people that have influenced your life because of their intimate knowledge of and relationship with Christ? Respond below.

PRAYER
Heavenly Father, thank You for the people who have taught me all about You. Help me know what it means to know You intimately. Amen.

DISCIPLING OTHERS
Week 42: *Show Mercy*
BECOMING DIVIDED
Jude 18–19

They said to you, "In the last times there will be scoffers who will follow their own ungodly desires." These are the people who divide you, who follow mere natural instincts and do not have the Spirit.

I graduated from a major liberal arts university in Georgia in 1974. I was amazed at the teachers who used their lecture halls as an opportunity to question, scoff at, and even attack Christianity. As a young believer who had been raised in a Christian family and actively involved in a church, I experienced for the first time attacks against my faith and my knowledge of God that became personal. It was not a fun experience, but one that helped me cement my own belief in Christ.

Jude reminded his readers that the apostles had warned them about the attacks that would come against the church and its believers. He also understood how difficult and potentially dangerous those attacks could be. Attacks could divide believers, weakening the body as a result. And the attacks would come from those who did not know Christ. It is from that ignorance that these could do the most damage.

What stories have you heard (or events you've experienced) when a local church became divided because of attacks from outside? How could the church have withstood the attack without becoming divided? Record your thoughts below.

PRAYER
Heavenly Father, teach me to withstand attack, criticism, and ridicule because of my faith. Help me to love those who attack. Amen.

DISCIPLING OTHERS
Week 42: *Show Mercy*
BUILDING UP THE BODY — Jude 20

> But you, dear friends, by building yourselves up in your most holy faith and praying in the Holy Spirit.

Years ago, I served at a church that became divided from within. The division didn't happen all at once, but grew over months and even years as issues became more polarizing. In the end, the congregation was divided almost in half. After one particularly difficult vote, many left the church to begin a new congregation. But the division left its mark on both congregations. The believers on both sides took years to recover emotionally and spiritually from the split of the congregation.

Jude could see the damage that would be done to local congregations and to the cause of Christ if outside forces created division with the church. He recognized the importance of working together to build up the body rather than allowing outsiders to trigger internal struggles. Paul explained the challenge this way, "From him the whole body, joined and held together by every supporting ligament, grows and builds itself up in love, as each part does its work" (Ephesians 4:16). Jude exhorted his readers to build up the body using their faith and praying to the Holy Spirit.

How do you personally work to build up your church and its members? How are you supportive of the work of the church? Respond below.

PRAYER
Heavenly Father, show me how I am supportive of my church. Convict when I am not. Help me understand what the body can be when we work together as believers. Amen.

Week 42: *Show Mercy*
IN SAFEKEEPING
Jude 21

Keep yourselves in God's love as you wait for the mercy of our Lord Jesus Christ to bring you to eternal life.

Shortly before my father passed away, he showed us a bag in which he had saved every letter he had received from my mother when they were dating. He needed help in preserving these memories because he wanted to give it to my mom as a gift. His health wouldn't allow him to complete the project, so our family jumped in, sorting, organizing, and preserving each document that was so important to him.

The NIV uses the word *keep*, which can also be translated as "preserve" to begin this verse. The word "preserve" means to "keep something safe from harm or destruction." The emphasis is placed on safely keeping something we already have. The word is an active verb, indicating intentional effort and attention. We preserve—protect, save, maintain, keep—the things we most value. Jude reminds us that it is our responsibility to preserve God's love as the thing we most value.

What things have you saved over your lifetime? Why are these worth keeping? Where do you keep them? Respond below. Then, compare your list with the things of faith you hold dear. How do you preserve those spiritual treasures in your life?

PRAYER
Heavenly Father, thank You for loving me. Help me learn how to safely preserve the things from You as the most important things in my life. Amen.

DISCIPLING OTHERS
Week 42: *Show Mercy*

HAVE MERCY

Jude 22–23

Be merciful to those who doubt; save others by snatching them from the fire; to others show mercy, mixed with fear—hating even the clothing stained by corrupted flesh.

We've been married almost forty years. The years together have taught us how to love and how to fight, how to express ourselves, and how to forgive each other. They've taught us how to work and play together as a couple, how to respect the personhood of the other, and how to parent our children. And they've taught us about the depth of God's love through our love for each other, our children, and our grandchildren. No marriage survives as long as ours has without learning to forgive, to accept, to respect, and to show mercy. Those are all things that we first experience through God's grace.

Jude completed his letter by describing how believers should respond to those who were being pulled into the false teachings. Believers were to work to strengthen the body as well as their own faith in the face of opposition and falsehood. However, their response to those who had not been able to stand firm should be one of love and mercy. Jude described several groups of people who had been hurt by these teachings. Some believers had become doubtful of their faith and now waivered in their beliefs. Others had never received salvation and the situation was urgent. Still others, through false teachings, had become guilty of immoral actions. Jude's very words demonstrate how serious the situation had become: *snatching...from fire; corrupted flesh*. For Jude, each group required its own brand of mercy.

The word "mercy" includes elements of compassion, kindness, and sympathy. Each of these characteristics can be difficult to express when we feel attacked or ridiculed. How have you been able to demonstrate mercy to hurt someone who has hurt you or someone close to you? How does the ability to show true mercy to another demonstrate the depth of the mercy God has shown you? Respond below.

PRAYER

Heavenly Father, help me to not become defensive when I feel attacked for my faith in You. Help me show Your love and mercy to those who seem the hardest to love. Amen.

THE BRIDGE TO MISSIONS
Week 43: *Reason Together*

SENSELESS
Isaiah 1:2-3

Hear me, you heavens! Listen, earth! For the LORD has spoken: "I reared children and brought them up, but they have rebelled against me. The ox knows its master, the donkey its owner's manger, but Israel does not know, my people do not understand."

In Disney's movie *The Lion King*, young Simba is convinced by his evil uncle Scar that he is responsible for his father's death. In fear of what will become of him, Simba flees, meets Timon and Pumba, and adopts their philosophy of *hakuna matata*, having "no worries." As a mature lion, his father appears to him in a vision and exhorts Simba with the words, "Remember who you are." For Simba, this means he has to return home and overthrow Scar, taking his rightful place as king of Pride Rock.

Our predicament is similar to Simba's. Sin has convinced us to flee the Father and convinced us to fight against His urgings to return in order to persist in our rebellion. As a result, we demonstrate even less sense than an ox or a donkey who clearly know who their master is. These senseless animals obey their masters; we wage war against and resist ours. The Spirit urges us to remember the purpose for which we were made—for a relationship with the Father through Jesus Christ.

Take a few minutes to examine your life. Is the Spirit urging you to wave the white flag on any form of rebellion in your life? Respond below.

PRAYER
Heavenly Father, thank You that You have made me for a relationship with You. Help me to give up any areas of rebellion in my life. Amen.

THE BRIDGE TO MISSIONS
Week 43: *Reason Together*
TRAIN WRECKS
Isaiah 1:5-6

Why should you be beaten anymore? Why do you persist in rebellion? Your whole head is injured, your whole heart afflicted. From the sole of your foot to the top of your head there is no soundness—only wounds and welts and open sores, not cleansed or bandaged or soothed with olive oil.

We have all watched as people we cared about laid waste to their own lives and the lives of those closest to them. From our perspective, their destructive behavior is overwhelmingly obvious. While the consequences of their actions come as no surprise to us, those consequences seem to surprise those in the midst of that destructive behavior. For us, the warning signs were obvious.

However, when we honestly evaluate our own lives, particularly in our relationship with God, we find we are often guilty of the same stubborn, senseless rebellion. We know that we are living contrary to the standards and purposes of God, but we persist in that behavior for some reason. When the consequences of our sin hit us, be it relational difficulties, financial troubles, whatever, we are genuinely surprised and accuse God of being unfaithful to us. In these situations, the problem is not God's faithfulness but our faithfulness to Him. Our sin has thoroughly corrupted us to the extent that we do not want to heed God's commandments.

Have you experienced the comprehensive consequences of sin? How can you guard from experiencing it again? Respond below.

PRAYER
Heavenly Father, thank You that You offer grace to me even after I stubbornly resist You. Help my heart to be soft to Your truth at all times. Amen.

THE BRIDGE TO MISSIONS
Week 43: *Reason Together*
ABHORRANT WORSHIP
Isaiah 1:13-14

Stop bringing meaningless offerings! Your incense is detestable to me. New Moons, Sabbaths and convocations—I cannot bear your worthless assemblies. Your New Moon feasts and your appointed festivals I hate with all my being. They have become a burden to me; I am weary of bearing them.

Imagine for a second that you are married. You remember a time in the past when you felt a deep connection with your spouse. You shared laughs, trials, and triumphs together, and genuinely enjoyed the other's company. In fact, the times that you spent with your spouse were the highlights of your week. When you had a tough day, you could think of nothing better than getting home and simply being with your spouse. Somewhere along the way that sense of connection dissipated. You still do all the things you used to do, but now it's just the pattern of life you follow. There is no real sense of joy in spending time with your spouse. You'll still plan dates and watch your favorite movies together, but oftentimes you would rather be by yourself.

Sadly, this later state of affairs is the way in which many of us approach our relationship with God. Prayer and Bible study—things that once brought so much life and joy—become drudgery and obligations that we must fulfill. Gathering for worship feels like an inconvenience. We would prefer to sleep in rather than gather and worship. The Lord's pronouncement for people who worship Him out of a sense of going through the motions is shocking: "Your worship is burdensome to me and I hate it."

Are you going through the motions in any aspect in your relationship with God? Is your relationship with God as vibrant as you would like it to be? Why?

PRAYER
Heavenly Father, revive me. May my worship of You be genuine and true at all times. Amen.

THE BRIDGE TO MISSIONS
Week 43: *Reason Together*
DISCONNECT   Isaiah 1:15-17

When you spread out your hands in prayer, I hide my eyes from you; even when you offer many prayers, I am not listening. Your hands are full of blood! Wash and make yourselves clean. Take your evil deeds out of my sight; stop doing wrong. Learn to do right; seek justice. Defend the oppressed. Take up the cause of the fatherless; plead the case of the widow.

The idea that God hears our prayers is a constant reminder that brings peace in the midst of the most difficult periods of life. We love the idea of being able to access God at any time and relish being assured that God not only hears our prayers, but loves to hear and respond to them.

As comforting as this thought is, it is not always true. God's people can find themselves opposing God's purposes by their conduct. When we find ourselves opposing God's purposes with our conduct, God warns us that He will not hear our prayers until our conduct matches our calling. Sometimes the prayer that is most appropriate is not the prayer of supplication or intercession. Rather, God most wants to hear a humble prayer of repentance that acknowledges our dependence on His grace and that we have represented the cause of our God well. God is not honored in our lip service or in our flippant acknowledgement of His work in our lives. God desires a people whose pattern of life matches the pattern of a redeemed heart.

Is there a disconnect between the redemption you profess and your pattern of life that you need to confess? Respond below.

PRAYER
Heavenly Father, help me to connect the grace and mercy You have shown me to my actions today. Amen.

THE BRIDGE TO MISSIONS
Week 43: *Reason Together*
A DOUBLE EDGED PROMISE — Isaiah 1:18-20

"Come now, let us settle the matter," says the Lord. "Though your sins are like scarlet, they shall be as white as snow; though they are red as crimson, they shall be like wool. If you are willing and obedient, you will eat the good things of the land; but if you resist and rebel, you will be devoured by the sword." For the mouth of the Lord has spoken.

In the *X-Men* movies and comics, Professor Charles Xavier (Professor X) and Eric Lecher (Magneto) are good friends who have very different ideas of how history should play out. Professor X envisions a day in which humans and mutants, those with super powers, can live peacefully side-by-side. Magneto envisions a day when mutants will overthrow the plague of humanity in a glorious revolution resulting in man's subservience to mutants. Professor X finds himself opposing his good friend at every turn while simultaneously pleading with him to abandon his militant hopes and embrace the way of peace. Until he does, Professor X and his friends will fight against Magneto and his associates. Professor X offers peace but promises consequences for persistent stubbornness.

Similarly, God promises us the opportunity to lay down our arms and embrace peace with Him. He offers the opportunity for our sins to be washed away, and our wrongs to be wiped out. However, if we choose to persist in our rebellion and sin, God promises that He will oppose us. We will miss His blessing and His good purposes for our lives. He offers us peace. But consequences are prepared if we reject His offer.

Have you experienced the consequences of persistent stubbornness in your walk with the Lord? What consequences did you face? How did you make your way back to God? Respond below.

PRAYER
Heavenly Father, forgive me for the times I reject Your offer of grace. Make my heart tender to Your correction in all circumstances. Amen.

THE BRIDGE TO MISSIONS
Week 44: *Righteous Wrath*

A GREAT EQUALIZER — Isaiah 24:1-2

See, the LORD is going to lay waste the earth and devastate it; he will ruin its face and scatter its inhabitants—it will be the same for priest as for people, for the master as for his servant, for the mistress as for her servant, for seller as for buyer, for borrower as for lender, for debtor as for creditor.

Human societies are always characterized by what differentiates us from other societies. Our social, economic, and political relationships are structured in such a way to give definition to relationships and to define roles and/or expectations. Unfortunately, these stratifications sometimes bring about inequities in opportunity—providing opportunities for those in positions of power or authority to take advantage of those lower than them. Those on the bottom end of these relationships often lament over the unfairness of the hand that has been dealt them.

A day is coming in which all of the classifications by which we divide ourselves will be rendered moot. God has promised that a day of reckoning is coming as long as humanity persists in our sin and rebellion. This thought is important to understand as affirmation of the holiness and justice of God in His judgment against sin. Since we are all guilty of rebellion against God, God's judgment of our sin is the great equalizer of humanity. All of our perceived and real differences, all societal stratifications, are rendered moot when God judges us for our sin.

Have you ever thought that your position or importance excuses your sin? How could that be rationalized? What is required in taking personal responsibility for your sin, regardless of your position or societal level? Respond below.

PRAYER
Heavenly Father, forgive me for the times I think I am above Your justice. Help me to have a humble estimation of myself. Amen.

THE BRIDGE TO MISSIONS
Week 44: *Righteous Wrath*
COMPREHENSIVE CORRUPTION — Isaiah 24:5-6a

The earth is defiled by its people; they have disobeyed the laws, violated the statutes and broken the everlasting covenant. Therefore a curse consumes the earth; its people must bear their guilt. Therefore earth's inhabitants are burned up, and very few are left.

In C.S. Lewis' *The Lion, The Witch, and the Wardrobe*, three children from England are magically transported from England to the kingdom of Narnia. In spite of all its enchantment, it becomes painfully obvious that Narnia is under a spell from a great witch. This witch has spies everywhere who report any rumblings of rebellion. She is greatly powerful. In fact, since her reign was inaugurated, the entire kingdom of Narnia had been in a constant state of winter. The corruption of the land was so comprehensive that the natural systems of the world even succumbed to deterioration.

In this respect our world is similar to Narnia. We have come under the spell and influence of sin. The result of our sin has far-reaching consequences that affect the very fabric of our being. Our relational patterns experience undue emotional and psychological turmoil. Even the natural ebbs and flows of life speak to the deterioration of life the way God intended. All of this is due to the effects of humanity's sin. We have brought this about. We deserve all the difficulty we experience in this world and far worse because we have rebelled against God, determined to be our own masters rather than submitting to His good, life-giving ways.

How have you seen the consequences of sin play out in your relationships or in natural occurrences? Describe those below.

PRAYER
Heavenly Father, forgive me for how I have perpetuated the patterns of sin and rebellion in the world. Thank You for the grace that you have shown me. Amen.

THE BRIDGE TO MISSIONS
Week 44: *Righteous Wrath*
GOODNESS IN JUDGMENT — Isaiah 24:14-15

They raise their voices, they shout for joy; from the west they acclaim the LORD's majesty. Therefore in the east give glory to the LORD; exalt the name of the LORD, the God of Israel, in the islands of the sea.

That God judges sin and deals with it so harshly is actually a good thing. Sin destroys...harms...subverts...perverts. If God did not act against sinful actions, we would have serious grounds to doubt His goodness. The fact that God is patient in executing His wrath in light of the serious, harmful nature of sin is more astounding than the fact that He does take action against it.

This knowledge of God provides grounds for His followers to continue to praise Him in light of His judgment against sin. Though we may not completely understand why God has chosen to take action at the particular time, we know that God has provided ample opportunity for repentance. Further, God's judgment demonstrates the weight that human action possesses. If our actions did not have the possibility for eternal significance, then God could be a passive spectator. God's judgment demonstrates that He is actively involved in the world and will set out to correct actions that destroy others and undermine His purposes. We do not have to like the fact that others have suffered, but we should be thankful that God cares for His creation. We should praise God that He forbore His wrath for so long and that His goodness requires Him to oppose the harmful effects of sin and rebellion.

Have you ever praised God for His judgment of sin? Do so below.

PRAYER
Heavenly Father, thank You that You oppose the things that destroy me and destroy others. Help me to see Your goodness in the midst of Your judgment. Amen.

THE BRIDGE TO MISSIONS
Week 44: *Righteous Wrath*
NO HIDING
Isaiah 24:17-18

Terror and pit and snare await you, people of the earth. Whoever flees at the sound of terror will fall into a pit; whoever climbs out of the pit will be caught in a snare. The floodgates of the heavens are opened, the foundations of the earth shake.

We've all heard stories of people who have runaway in hopes of finding a better life or avoiding consequences of their actions. Even more surprising, some people convince themselves they can escape the judgment of God. Either by cunning or running, they are convinced that if God ever does act against sin and rebellion, they will somehow be able to escape God's action.

This error is two-fold. First, God will most definitely act against sin and rebellion in judgment. Though we are uncomfortable with the thought, God's Word repeatedly demonstrates to us that God does periodically take decisive action against sin in the world and the sin of His people. The cross of Christ is the perfect demonstration of God's judgment of sin in the world. The cross demonstrates the gravity of humanity's sin and the extent to which God will go to deal with our sin.

Second, when God does judge sin, whether it be in a particular instance of judgment or in God's final judgment of sin, there will be no escape for those who are the objects of God's wrath. When God determines to judge sin, He does not relent and He is not so bereft of power as to be unable to accomplish what He has determined to do. The most cunning or strongest person is powerless to escape God's judgment when it falls.

What does God's judgment mean to you? To our world? What should our response as believers be to the knowledge of God's coming judgment?

PRAYER
Heavenly Father, forgive me for times that I have taken Your judgment lightly. May knowledge of Your power lead me to worship You. Amen.

THE BRIDGE TO MISSIONS
Week 44: *Righteous Wrath*

NO COMPARISON   Isaiah 24:23

The moon will be dismayed, the sun ashamed; for the LORD Almighty will reign on Mount Zion and in Jerusalem, and before its elders—with great glory.

In the story of *Robin Hood*, King George leaves England to fight in the Crusades. While he is gone, Prince John sets up a false kingdom. Though John's kingdom is false, it has real power. John uses this power to make life difficult for his subjects. In the movie's final scene, as John is about to have Robin Hood executed for crimes against his false kingdom, King George returns. King George spares Robin Hood and goes about restoring his kingdom. This process of restoration includes punishing Prince John for his rebellion and putting the once "begrudgingly" revered monarch into his proper place of humility, especially in comparison to King George's exalted status as true king.

Similarly, God's final judgment of sin will end with all sinful patterns in the world being corrected. The first step in this action will be in restoring true, proper order in mankind's pattern of worship. All of the false idols and distractions that plagued mankind will be overthrown and judged. Israel's neighbors worshipped the sun and the moon. God's final judgment will involve a humbling of even these revered bodies. Even the sun and the moon will bow down to their Creator because, after He takes His rightful place, His glory will far surpass anything that they are capable of.

Have you revered the creation over the Creator? How? Respond below.

PRAYER
Heavenly Father, please grant me a glimpse of Your glory. Remind me that Your name and renown is far higher than anything else that I could live for. Amen.

THE BRIDGE TO MISSIONS
Week 45: *Quick Grace*
GOD'S LONGING
Isaiah 30:18

Yet the LORD longs to be gracious to you; therefore he will rise up to show you compassion. For the LORD is a God of justice. Blessed are all who wait for him!

Have you ever gone an abnormal amount of time without food? Your body begins to physiologically long for food. It needs it to survive. You begin to imagine what the texture and flavor of your favorite food feels and tastes like on your tongue. You may fantasize about eating to the point that everything reminds you of the fact that you need to eat. Boxes can look like cheeseburgers or vans like sub sandwiches. A strong compulsion may overtake you to drop everything you're doing and go find food at that very instant.

The Lord longs to be gracious to His people. He yearns for it. He desires it above all else. His judgment is always a last resort, an action He takes when we persist again and again in stubbornness against His calls to repentance and life. In the same way that a starving man yearns for a morsel of bread or a drop of water, the Lord yearns to show grace, mercy, and kindness to His people. Those who allow the Lord to demonstrate this mercy and kindness towards them find that, in spite of the difficulties of their circumstances, He has been there all along, compassionately and lovingly guiding them through. Hindsight gives light to the truth that the Lord blesses those who wait on Him.

Are you are facing a difficult situation? Remember that the Lord longs to show you grace in the midst of your struggle. Below, consider how that grace can help you through this time.

PRAYER
Heavenly Father, thank You that You desire above all else to show me grace because I belong to You. Help me to experience the blessing of waiting on You in the midst of my struggle. Amen.

_____

_____

_____

_____

_____

THE BRIDGE TO MISSIONS
Week 45: *Quick Grace*
TURBO BOOSTED Isaiah 30:19b

How gracious he will be when you cry for help! As soon as he hears, he will answer you.

Growing up, I loved playing Super Mario Kart. The key to a good race in Mario Kart was timing the start perfectly. The Koopa Troopa would fly down in his cloud with the start light hanging from a fishing pole with the light on red. The light changed to yellow, and then, in the next instant, to green. If you timed the start correctly you burst from the starting line ahead of everyone else with a quick turbo boost and never looked back.

God stands at the ready to show us grace. All He is waiting for is our admission that we need His grace. As long as we persist in our stubbornness in thinking that we have everything under control apart from the care and oversight of God, He will allow us to experience the fruit of such a lifestyle. When we humbly admit that we are dependent on the Lord in all things and that we need and desire His grace to sustain us, the Lord springs to action. When the Lord feels far away, it is because we have not come to Him humbly and asked for His intervention.

Is there any matter that you have hesitated to go to the Lord with? What is keeping you from experiencing God's grace in your situation? Respond below.

PRAYER
Heavenly Father, thank You for promising to answer when I call to You humbly. Help me to experience Your grace through humility. Amen.

_____

_____

_____

_____

_____

_____

THE BRIDGE TO MISSIONS
Week 45: *Quick Grace*
REASSURANCE
Isaiah 30:21

Whether you turn to the right or to the left, your ears will hear a voice behind you, saying, "This is the way; walk in it."

Everyone longs for reassurance. Our desire for reassurance is often at its height when we make changes in life or embark on a new task. When I first became a Christian, the Lord led me to give up two strong friendships that would have been a hindrance to my growth in my new faith. Giving up those friendships led to some lonely times in which I questioned the wisdom of my decision. I desperately wanted to know that I had done the right thing and that my sense of loneliness would somehow improve.

The Lord promises that when we center ourselves to live according to His way, He will go with us and provide timely reassurance. No matter what pathway the Lord leads you down, He knows your heart, your struggles, and your needs even better than you know them yourself. He knows the perfect moment at which you need a word of encouragement in order to persevere in the course on which He has led you. In these times, the Lord's whisper of reassurance is the greatest comfort that we can know. We simply must be quiet enough to hear Him.

How do you need to make time to be silent and receive the Lord's reassurance? What difference does making that time a priority in your life make?

PRAYER
Heavenly Father, thank You that You reassure me when You lead me down a path. Help me to hear Your whisper of reassurance. Amen.

THE BRIDGE TO MISSIONS
Week 45: *Quick Grace*
GRACE'S EFFECT　　　　　　　　　　Isaiah 30:22

Then you will desecrate your idols overlaid with silver and your images covered with gold; you will throw them away like a menstrual cloth and say to them, "Away with you!"

In a lot of ways, my salvation experience was unremarkable. I was fourteen years old and had not done anything that would be considered as truly "bad." I was an average kid with average fourteen-year-old kid problems. What I remember most about my salvation experience was the ride home after that church service. We lived in the country and our church was nestled in a picturesque valley. As I rode home in the back seat, I felt like I was seeing it all for the first time. As the week unfolded, I found I thought about relationships differently, made decisions based on a new set of priorities, and generally had a new frame of mind.

Such is the effect of a true experience with the grace of God. Some with more dramatic testimonies recount experiences of throwing away old instruments of sin, be they bottles of liquor or magazines, or a million other things. In frontier mission areas, accounts of new converts burning or throwing away idols or instruments of their former religion are common. The only impetus for such a dramatic change of lifestyle, behavior, or mind-set is an experience with the grace of God. When we truly experience God's grace, change is unavoidable. We cannot help but want to rid ourselves of the things that we now understand to have separated us from our King. We finally comprehend that sin keeps us from God, and God is the greatest good that we can have.

How did your salvation experience change the way you viewed your life and your relationships? How would you explain that experience to a non-believer?

PRAYER
Heavenly Father, thank You for the truth that Your grace has changed me. Help me to continue to be conformed to the likeness of Your Son through Your grace. Amen.

_____

_____

_____

_____

THE BRIDGE TO MISSIONS
Week 45: *Quick Grace*
RESOLUTION
Isaiah 30:26

The moon will shine like the sun, and the sunlight will be seven times brighter, like the light of seven full days, when the LORD **binds up the bruises of his people and heals the wounds he inflicted.**

Every plotline to a story develops in similar ways. It begins with an introductory period in which the characters and players are introduced and the reader develops an attachment to them. A problem is introduced that makes things difficult for the characters involved and through which they struggle for the majority of the story. Finally, some form of resolution is provided. In the stories we most love, the resolution solves the major problems and leaves the audience with a sense of relief. The danger has passed; the characters we love will be fine.

God's story develops similarly. God created mankind in His image and lived in perfect harmony with them in the Garden. Mankind, tempted by the enemy, rebelled against God's ways. The story of humanity has become a testimony to the compressive and damaging effects of sin. Fortunately, resolution to the problem of strained relations between God and man has been initiated in the person and work of Christ. A day is coming when this resolution will reach its climax and God will finally, decisively, put an end to sin. In that day, we will fully experience what it means to be God's people and to live under His blessing and presence forever. Our wounds will be at last fully healed and the presence of our God will be our joy forever.

Spend some time thanking God for victory in His presence that we will experience. Then, record your thanks below.

PRAYER
Heavenly Father, thank You that You have acted against the effects of sin in the world through Your Son. Help me to find relief in Your presence. Amen.

THE BRIDGE TO MISSIONS
Week 46: *Safe and Secure*
A SOLID REPUTATION
Isaiah 43:1b-2

Do not fear, for I have redeemed you; I have summoned you by name; you are mine. When you pass through the waters, I will be with you; and when you pass through the rivers, they will not sweep over you. When you walk through the fire, you will not be burned; the flames will not set you ablaze.

Life can be full of trials and tribulations that shake us to our core. Whether it is an unexpected medical bill that we aren't sure how we will pay or the emotional and psychological strain of a broken relationship, the struggle can at times feel overwhelming. We sometimes doubt whether we will be able to make it through the trial.

Waters and fire are symbolic of great struggles that people of God have faced before. The "waters" reference the people of Israel passing through the waters of the Red Sea in their flight from Egypt. The "fires" reference both Elijah's showdown with the prophets of Baal at Mt. Carmel and the fires of the furnace that Shadrach, Meshach, and Abednego were cast into for their obedience to God. In all of these cases, God delivered those who trusted in Him. Israel passed through the sea on dry ground. Elijah demonstrated to the people that the Lord was the true God and not Baal. Shadrach, Meshach, and Abednego proved that their God could deliver them from any trial, even being cast into a fiery furnace. God has demonstrated His deliverance to those who trust in Him.

How can you take comfort in the testimony of those who have gone before you that God delivers even out of the greatest trials? Respond below.

PRAYER
Heavenly Father, You deliver those who trust in You. Help me to remember this even when I am experiencing trials. Amen.

THE BRIDGE TO MISSIONS
Week 46: *Safe and Secure*
PRECIOUS IN GOD'S SIGHT Isaiah 43:3-4

For I am the LORD your God, the Holy One of Israel, your Savior; I give Egypt for your ransom, Cush and Seba in your stead. Since you are precious and honored in my sight, and because I love you, I will give people in exchange for you, nations in exchange for your life.

In the movie *The Pirates of the Caribbean*, Captain Jack Sparrow constantly searched for some kind of treasure. Though he demonstrated moments of concern for others, his overriding concern was his acquisition of some form of treasure or possession. Because of this, he placed others, even those he cared about, in a variety of sticky predicaments. His concern was not for people, but for possessions.

God's concern is for His people. As children of God through His grace, we are precious and highly valued in His sight. He works our situations out in such a way that He protects us and guards us from danger. Because He loves us and has redeemed us, He orchestrates events in such a way that we are safe in His arms. Though we experience trials and tribulations in this life, God promises us that He protects us from unnecessary difficulties and struggles out of His great love for us.

How has God delivered you from unnecessary trails? What have you learned about God through your experiences? Respond below.

PRAYER
Heavenly Father, You have redeemed me. You love me greatly. Thank You that Your concern is for me and that You keep me safe from meaningless sufferings. Amen.

THE BRIDGE TO MISSIONS
Week 46: *Safe and Secure*
SECURITY   Isaiah 43:5a

Do not be afraid, for I am with you.

When my wife gets scared, her first reaction is to grab me and not let go. I refer to these grasps as "kung-fu death locks." It doesn't matter if I struggle to get free. She will not be letting go until she feels secure and calm again. For her, security rests in knowing that I am right there with her.

The Lord longs for His people to cling to Him in much the same way. He never promises His people that we will not experience difficulty or trials. Instead, He promises His presence in the midst of difficulty and trials. In His presence is our only basis for peace and security in the midst of our circumstances. When we cling to the Lord through His Word, through prayer, and through committing to live according to His way even when things are difficult, He grants us peace that surpasses all understanding. When the world is caving in around us and we rest secure in the presence of our God, God's people become a powerful testimony to the rest of the world that struggles to find peace and security even when things are going well.

Do you need to find rest in the presence of God in any circumstance that you are facing? Record your need for God's rest below.

PRAYER
Heavenly Father, You are my only basis for peace. Help me to resolve to cling to You in the midst of difficult circumstances and experience Your peace in them. Amen.

THE BRIDGE TO MISSIONS
Week 46: *Safe and Secure*
THE PRIVILEDGE OF KNOWING Isaiah 43:10

"You are my witnesses," declares the LORD, "and my servant whom I have chosen, so that you may know and believe me and understand that I am he. Before me no god was formed, nor will there be one after me."

If we are asked what the greatest thing about our salvation is, most of us will respond with some benefit that we have received as a result. We like knowing that our sins are forgiven, that we will go to heaven when we die, that we have peace in this life, or a host of other benefits. These are certainly good things that those who experience salvation undeniably receive, but words from God's own mouth refute the idea that these are the greatest aspects of receiving His salvation.

According to the words of the Lord, the greatest elements of a person's salvation is found in the fact that the redeemed know, believe in, and understand the fact that the Lord is the only true God. The greatest benefits of salvation are not centered on what an individual receives. Instead, they are centered on coming to know God. Only those who have been redeemed by God truly know Him. Only those whom God has saved have a true belief of His nature as a loving, merciful God. Only those who understand His ways know with certainty that He is the greatest possible deity. There simply is no comparison in any other system of faith or philosophy to compare with the greatness of our God.

Below, record your praise to God for the privilege of knowing Him, the only true God, through His grace.

PRAYER
Heavenly Father, You have created and saved me to know You. Thank You for the privilege of having a relationship with You by grace through faith. Amen.

THE BRIDGE TO MISSIONS
Week 46: *Safe and Secure*

NOT ALONE — Isaiah 43:11-13

"I, even I, am the LORD, and apart from me there is no savior. I have revealed and saved and proclaimed—I, and not some foreign god among you. You are my witnesses," declares the LORD, "that I am God. Yes, and from ancient days I am he. No one can deliver out of my hand. When I act, who can reverse it?"

Human beings have a remarkable ability to overlook truths and realities that were once obvious to us. We tend to frame stories and memories in such a manner as to make ourselves look more favorable than we were in a particular instance. When it comes to matters of faith, once the euphoria of a spiritual high wears off, we tend to rationalize our experience in an attempt to help ourselves understand what really occurred. In the midst of all of this, the Lord often gets explained out of our stories.

The Lord calls us to remember His person and how He has acted on our behalf. He calls us to remember that He has saved us from our sin and from judgment that we deserve. He calls us to remember that He has made Himself known to us—the greatest benefit that we can receive from Him. Instead of rationalizing our experiences and attributing God's action to some other phenomenon or person, God calls us to be witnesses to His action in the world. The Lord is the one who controls all the events of our lives. Our rationalizations of His activity rob Him of the glory that He is due and subvert His purpose for us to be His witnesses in the world.

How can you consistently remind yourself of how God has acted on your behalf? Respond below.

PRAYER
Heavenly Father, You have saved me and revealed Yourself to me. Help me to never fail to testify to Your greatness and mercy in any circumstance. Amen.

THE BRIDGE TO MISSIONS
Week 47: *Suffering Servant*

ULTIMATE REJECTION
Isaiah 53:3

He was despised and rejected by mankind, a man of suffering, and familiar with pain. Like one from whom people hide their faces he was despised, and we held him in low esteem.

In the *X-Men* movies and comics, the good guys struggle because humanity despises and rejects them, despite the fact that they are working towards bettering the condition of humanity by combating evil. They are labeled "mutants" and are considered to be a danger to humanity that must be contained and looked upon with derision.

Christ faced a similar predicament. Mankind considered His message and His lifestyle of so little importance that they completely and utterly rejected Him. Christ knew what it was like to experience extreme suffering. He experienced real pain as a result of the emotional and psychological turmoil by the way humanity treated Him. Instead of considering Him worthy of their attention, mankind treated Him as a pariah and a social outcast. Humanity found a way to marginalize His message and to refute His character instead of recognizing Him as the messenger of God's salvation. In this way, Christ is able to relate to those among us who have similar stories of rejection and pain. Though no other person may completely understand how we feel when we are rejected by others, Christ knows this pain better than anyone else.

How can you take comfort in knowing that Christ can sympathize with rejection you have experienced? Respond below.

PRAYER
Heavenly Father, You have experienced pain and rejection to an ultimate degree. Help me to find comfort in Your person when I experience similar struggles. Amen.

THE BRIDGE TO MISSIONS
Week 47: *Suffering Servant*
THE PRICE OF PEACE Isaiah 53:4-5

Surely he took up our pain and bore our suffering, yet we considered him punished by God, stricken by him, and afflicted. But he was pierced for our transgressions, he was crushed for our iniquities; the punishment that brought us peace was on him, and by his wounds we are healed.

In C.S. Lewis' classic tale, *The Lion, The Witch, and the Wardrobe*, the three main characters find themselves deserving of the death penalty from the witch who rules the enchanted land of Narnia. The only way they are able to escape the consequences of their actions is when Aslan, the great lion, agrees to die in their place. He took their punishment. They were reprieved.

Christ took our place and paid a price we could not pay. We were guilty of sin and deserved the judgment and full wrath of God. Christ took our place and paid the price of our sin and rebellion for us. His reward for this action has been to be vilified and marginalized by the majority of mankind for centuries. However, the greatness of Christ lies in the fact that He did not take on our sin for our applause. He took on the consequences of our sin in order to bring us into a relationship with God, a relationship characterized by peace and wholeness. When we believe in the person and work of Christ, we are brought into peace with God. The wounds of our sin that have hurt us for so long begin to be healed and renewed.

What has been the healing impact of the work of Christ in your life? How can you explain that impact to someone who has not experienced it personally?

PRAYER
Heavenly Father, You sent Your son to pay a price I could not pay so that I may have a relationship with You. Help me to understand the greatness of the work of Christ in my life. Amen.

THE BRIDGE TO MISSIONS
Week 47: *Suffering Servant*

IN OUR PLACE   Isaiah 53:6

We all, like sheep, have gone astray, each of us has turned to our own way; and the Lord has laid on him the iniquity of us all.

In the movie *The Bourne Identity*, Jason Bourne awakes on a fishing vessel with no memory of how he got there or who he is. He quickly discovers that he is a wanted man being pursued by some mysterious group of people. The remainder of the movie depicts his struggle to understand who he is, how he got where he is, and how he can get out of his predicament.

When we come to Christ, we realize that our life before Christ was characterized by a great sense of disorientation. The moment we place our trust in Christ as our Savior, we gain a new understanding of just how lost we were. Remarkably, even though this lost-ness is natural, we struggle to understand how we got to that position. As we grow in our faith, we understand that our lost-ness and sense of disorientation was the result of our sin that separated us from God. We understand that we followed our own passions and desires and that this pursuit turned us away from God. We deserved death and the wrath of God. Thankfully, Christ took our sin upon Himself and made a way for us to enjoy peace with God.

Below, express your praise to God for the truth that Christ was our substitute on the cross.

PRAYER
Heavenly Father, You made a way for me to have a relationship with You through the work of Christ on the cross. Thank You for this truth. Amen.

_____

_____

_____

_____

_____

_____

THE BRIDGE TO MISSIONS
Week 47: *Suffering Servant*
TRIUMPH, NOT TRAGEDY — Isaiah 53:10

Yet it was the LORD's will to crush him and cause him to suffer, and though the LORD makes his life an offering for sin, he will see his offspring and prolong his days, and the will of the LORD will prosper in his hand.

We can be tempted to speak of the cross as if it were simply a great tragedy. While the events of the cross are heart-wrenching, and the details surrounding its legality or fairness can be rightfully questioned, to speak of the cross simply as a tragedy misses the point.

All along, the cross of Christ was the will of God. Christ had to suffer the injustice and indignity of the cross in order for salvation to be possible for all mankind. The events surrounding the cross are not pretty and will never evoke a pleasant feeling when we consider the immense suffering that Christ endured for us. However, the cross can only be seen as a tragedy when we separate the events of the cross from the resurrection of Christ. Christ's resurrection demonstrated God's approval of the work of Christ. Christ's death and resurrection ushered in the kingdom of God and made it possible for the will of God to be done on earth as it is in heaven. The cross is not a tragedy. The cross is the very purpose and will of God.

Below, describe the importance of the cross in your life. Think of those you know that have not yet discovered what the cross can do for them. Pray that God will give you an opportunity to share how the cross has changed you with these people.

PRAYER
Heavenly Father, thank You for the victory and glory of the cross. Help me to understand all that You accomplished for me there. Amen.

THE BRIDGE TO MISSIONS
Week 47: *Suffering Servant*

NOT THE END
Isaiah 53:12a

Therefore I will give him a portion among the great, and he will divide the spoils with the strong, because he poured out his life unto death, and was numbered with the transgressors.

If the cross is the end of God's story, then Christ's death can be spoken of as a great tragedy. If the cross is the end of the story, then Jesus was simply a good teacher who lived a good life and died an inglorious and untimely death.

But the cross is not the end of God's story. God raised Christ from the dead and gave Him "a portion among the great." Through the resurrection, God vindicated the work and message of Christ. Because Christ was faithful to the will of God by going to the cross and enduring its pain and suffering, God, in turn, raised Christ from the dead and validated the work He accomplished. The cross is not simply a symbolic understanding of redemption through suffering. Literally, Christ took on our sin. He "was numbered with the transgressors" and died a very real death. Similarly, the resurrection is not a symbol of experiencing vindication or of receiving new life. The resurrection is the historical occurrence that demonstrated God's approval and acceptance of the sacrifice of Jesus on our behalf.

Below, record God's story in your life. Then, prayerfully consider ways you can share that story with others.

PRAYER
Heavenly Father, You raised Christ and demonstrated Your acceptance and approval of His work on my behalf. Thank You for providing a way for me to have a relationship with You through Your Son. Amen.

THE BRIDGE TO MISSIONS
Week 48: *Free Future*

EXTREME MAKEOVER — Isaiah 65:17

"See, I will create new heavens and a new earth. The former things will not be remembered, nor will they come to mind."

I love the show *Extreme Makeover: Home Edition*. In the show, a family living in sub-standard housing is given a brand new home tailored to their specific circumstances and needs. However, for this new home to be constructed, the old home must be completely torn down and demolished. The new, more suitable home can only come about by the destruction of the old, poorly functioning home.

God will one day radically re-create the world. This world has been stained and tainted by the presence and prominence of sin and will not be suitable as a home for the redeemed of God. This thought is often difficult for us. Though we know that this world has been tainted by sin, we still enjoy some things here. Not everything is bad, so why would God destroy it all in favor of something new? The answer is that even the things that appear to be good here are not good in their highest forms. The world that God has created for His redeemed contains only the greatest good that we can experience. This world will be so good that we will not even remember the things in this world that we once enjoyed.

Below, reflect on this statement: The presence of God and the greatness of the new world He creates for us will far exceed any joy or peace we feel here.

PRAYER
Heavenly Father, You will one day put an end to the pain and suffering of this world. Thank You that You will provide a place of joy and peace for the redeemed for eternity. Amen.

THE BRIDGE TO MISSIONS
Week 48: *Free Future*

NO MORE TEARS
Isaiah 65:18-19

"But be glad and rejoice forever in what I will create, for I will create Jerusalem to be a delight and its people a joy. I will rejoice over Jerusalem and take delight in my people; the sound of weeping and of crying will be heard in it no more."

Tears let us know that things are not right. We cry when we are heartbroken because we aren't meant to experience deep hurt. We cry when plans are frustrated because we aren't meant to know despair and frustration. We cry over the sudden, untimely death of others because so much seems unfulfilled in their lives. Tears testify that things are not the way they are meant to be.

Tears will be absent in the new heaven and the new earth that God will create. All things will finally be set right. We will no longer have our hearts broken. We will no longer experience despair or frustration. We will no longer know the anguish of untimely death. In place of these experiences, we will know the joy and gladness of being in the presence of God forever. If tears are present in the new heaven and new earth, they will only be tears of joy at the fact that our hearts are finally at rest and peace eternally.

Below, describe how your eternal life will be different than your earthly life. Praise God for the promise of eternal peace and joy in His presence forever.

PRAYER
Heavenly Father, there will be no more tears of pain or suffering when I am in Your presence forever. Thank You that Your presence provides the fulfillment for all my longings and pains. Amen.

THE BRIDGE TO MISSIONS
Week 48: *Free Future*
ULTIMATE FULFILLMENT   Isaiah 65:22

No longer will they build houses and others live in them, or plant and others eat. For as the days of a tree, so will be the days of my people; my chosen ones will long enjoy the work of their hands.

One of the great indignities the Israelites experienced when they were exiled was that foreigners now occupied their houses and enjoyed the fruits of their labors. To them, this was a great injustice and was a direct assault on their status as the chosen people of God. We experience similar frustrations when we encounter injustice. We feel we should be able to enjoy the fruits of our labors. When we don't, it is a testimony that things are not as they are supposed to be.

In the kingdom of God, we will long enjoy the works of our hands. We will know the contentment that comes from a long life and the satisfaction of enjoying the labors of our works for a full lifetime. Heaven will not simply be a place in which we sing with a chorus of angels forever while floating on a cloud playing a harp. Heaven will be a place where we enjoy a life at union with God. We will enjoy the labors of our hands, meaning we will finally find satisfaction in the elements of day-to-day life while we live with God forever. Heaven will be life as it was meant to be before the effects of sin corrupted life on earth.

How does this understanding affect your perception of eternity? Respond below.

PRAYER
Heavenly Father, You have promised that I will enjoy Your presence forever. Help me to understand how to enjoy Your presence even in the mundane aspects of life. Amen.

THE BRIDGE TO MISSIONS
Week 48: *Free Future*
UNINTERRUPTED INTIMACY Isaiah 65:24

Before they call I will answer; while they are still speaking I will hear.

One of the joys of marriage is finding someone to be at one with for the rest of your life. As your understanding of and intimacy with the other increases, you find yourself finishing one another's sentences. You begin to gain an understanding of the way the other thinks and you can anticipate his or her words, sometimes even the quirks of expressions.

This will be the type of intimacy we will experience with God when we enjoy His presence forever in the new heaven and the new earth. Without the effects of sin and death separating us from our God, we will be able to enjoy such intimacy with God that our longings, needs, and desires will be immediately anticipated. How is this possible? Without the effects of sin and death, our desires, longings, and needs will be the same as our Father's. We will know full communion with God because the one thing that made such communion impossible in this life will finally be removed.

Below, express your thanks to God for the promise of uninterrupted fellowship with Him forever apart from the effects of sin and death.

PRAYER
Heavenly Father, You created me to be at one with You and one day I will enjoy this relationship in its fullness. Thank You for the greatness of this promise. Amen.

THE BRIDGE TO MISSIONS
Week 48: *Free Future*
ULTIMATE PEACE — Isaiah 65:25

"The wolf and the lamb will feed together, and the lion will eat straw like the ox, and dust will be the serpent's food. They will neither harm nor destroy on all my holy mountain," says the LORD.

On December 24, 1914, German and British troops were at a standstill in a trench-warfare battle common to World War I. Suddenly, the German troops stopped firing and started singing Christmas carols. British troops joined in the caroling and before long the two sides were swapping Christmas presents and playing soccer games. The unexpected truce ended when Christmas passed and the war trudged on for four more years.

Such stories resonate deep within us because we long for a world with no conflict. When the kingdom of God comes in its fullness, it will be characterized by complete and utter peace. Wars and strife between people will no longer exist in the presence of God. The level of peace we will enjoy will even extend to animals. Predatory relationships will cease. Animals that were once a danger to humanity will no longer be a threat. The presence of God in His kingdom will eliminate all elements of struggle and strife that were caused by the effects of sin in this world. Sin will be completely absent and so will strife.

Below, write your prayer of thanks to God for this promise of ultimate peace in His kingdom.

PRAYER
Heavenly Father, thank You for Your promise of ultimate peace in Your presence forever. Amen.

CONCLUSION

The journey of discipleship is one without end. Every day, we have the opportunity to learn more about God, to grow in our relationship with Him, to experience lives that are full of His blessing and worthy of His love. The journey of discipleship will not end with this life.

Our journey of discipleship also does not end with us. Jesus spoke of our responsibility for sharing our faith with others. The gospel of John records these words of Jesus, spoken to His disciples: "I no longer call you servants, because a servant does not know his master's business. Instead, I have called you friends, for everything that I learned from my Father I have made known to you. You did not choose me, but I chose you and appointed you so that you might go and bear fruit—fruit that will last—and so that whatever you ask in my name the Father will give you. This is my command: Love each other" (John 15:15–17). We cannot be disciples without bearing fruit...the fruit produced when others are brought to Christ and taught what that means.

In His final words to His disciples before He ascended into heaven, Jesus expressed the important role His disciples were to assume: "All authority in heaven and on earth has been given to me. Therefore go and make disciples of all nations, baptizing them in the name of the Father and of the Son and of the Holy Spirit, and teaching them to obey everything I have commanded you. And surely I am with you always, to the very end of the age" (Matthew 28:18–20).

May the journey continue...

WRITERS

Jenny Riddle wrote the devotions for Unit 3. Jenny has a Master of Divinity from the New Orleans Baptist Theological Seminary. God has given Jenny the skills and passion to proclaim His truth through writing. She and her husband, Stephen, are daily learning about the redemptive message of the gospel and their stewardship of His mercy as adoptive parents. She brings these passions and experiences to her devotions on *Using God's Gifts Wisely.*

Benjie Shaw wrote the devotions for Unit 4 and Unit 8. Benjie graduated with a Master of Divinity from the New Orleans Baptist Theological Seminary and has written for Life**Bible**Study. Benjie is passionate about studying the original language of the Bible as a way of connecting to God's Word. He loves helping young adults on their discipleship journeys. He brings his love for the Scripture, young adults, and discipleship to his devotions on *Acting Out Faith* and *The Bridge to Missions.*

Marilyn Stewart wrote the devotions for Unit 2 and Unit 5. Marilyn graduated with a Master of Divinity from Southwestern Baptist Theological Seminary. Her free-lance writing career took off after Hurricane Katrina as she reported in New Orleans for the Louisiana Baptist Convention and *The Baptist Message*, the newsjournal of Louisiana Southern Baptists. She currently writes a weekly column for *The Times–Picayune* in New Orleans and has written for numerous Christian resources. She brings a unique perspective to her devotions on *Holy Disciplines* and *Coming Back to God.*

Bob Williamson wrote the devotions for Unit 1, Unit 6, and Unit 7. Bob graduated from the University of Georgia with a degree in Forestry before completing a Master of Religious Education at The Southern Baptist Theological Seminary and a Doctorate in Educational Ministries at the New Orleans Baptist Theological Seminary. He is a certified arborist with his own tree farm and has served at the same church for over twenty years. He gets excited about watching things grow—both trees and disciples. He brings that passion to his devotions on *Living in Worship*, *Relating to Others*, and *Discipling Others.*

Editorial and Design Staff

Editor
Margie Williamson

Graphic Design
Jennifer Myers